Vietnam at the Crossroads

CHATHAM HOUSE PAPERS

An Asia-Pacific Programme Publication
Programme Director: Peter Ferdinand

The Royal Institute of International Affairs, at Chatham House in London, has provided an impartial forum for discussion and debate on current international issues for some 70 years. Its resident research fellows, specialized information resources, and range of publications, conferences, and meetings span the fields of international politics, economics, and security. The Institute is independent of government.

Chatham House Papers are short monographs on current policy problems which have been commissioned by the RIIA. In preparing the papers, authors are advised by a study group of experts convened by the RIIA, and publication of a paper indicates that the Institute regards it as an authoritative contribution to the public debate. The Institute does not, however, hold opinions of its own; the views expressed in this publication are the responsibility of the author.

CHATHAM HOUSE PAPERS

Vietnam at the Crossroads

Michael C. Williams

The Royal Institute of International Affairs

Pinter Publishers
London

© Royal Institute of International Affairs, 1992

First published in Great Britain in 1992 by
Pinter Publishers Limited
25 Floral Street, London WC2E 9DS

British Library Cataloguing in Publication Data

A CIP catalogue record for this book is available from the British Library

ISBN 1-85567-052-6 (Paperback)
      1-85567-051-8 (Hardback)

Reproduced from copy supplied by
Koinonia Limited
Printed and bound in Great Britain by
Biddles Ltd

CONTENTS

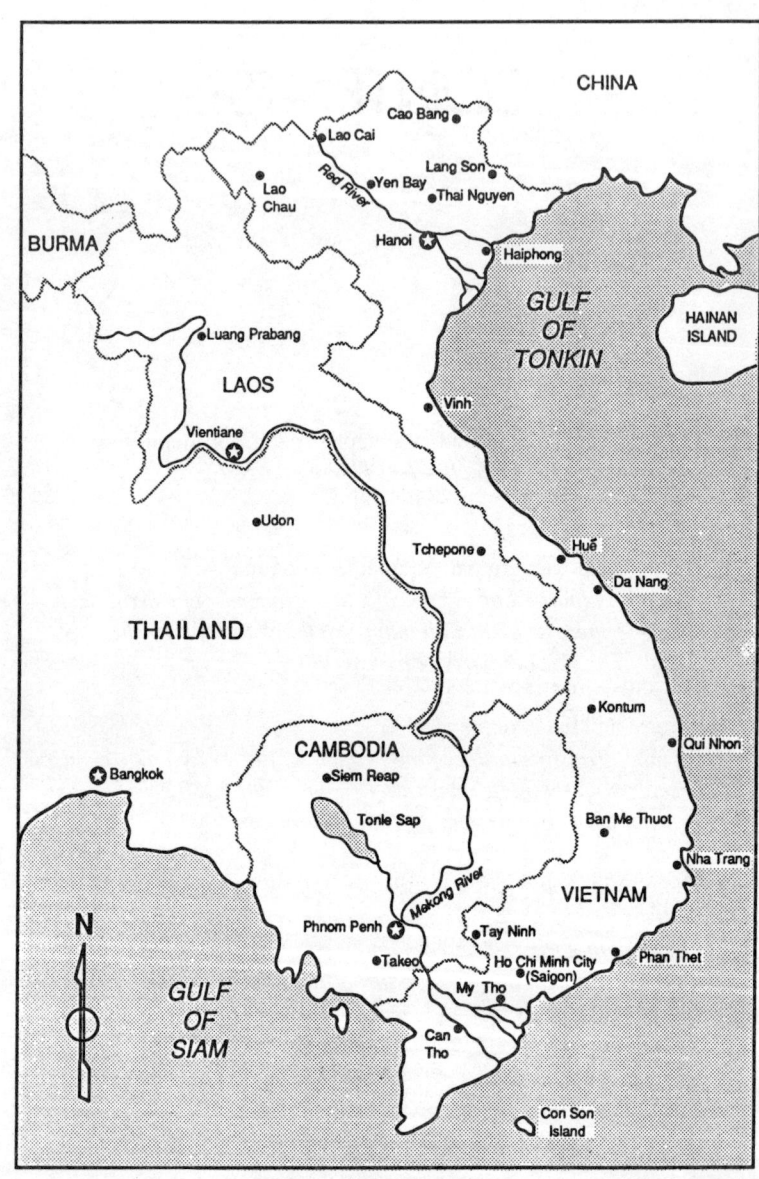

Courtesy of Ohio University Center for International Studies

Vietnam, Laos and Cambodia

ACKNOWLEDGMENTS

Unlike many Chatham House Papers, this study was not written in house. For their patience and forbearance while I took the odd week off to write, I would like to thank Basil Clarke, the Head of the BBC Far Eastern Service, and my colleagues on 'Dateline East Asia'. The suggestion for this study came from Peter Ferdinand, the Head of the Asia-Pacific Programme at Chatham House, and for his support throughout I am grateful. Drafts of the paper were discussed at Chatham House at two study group meetings in February 1992 and I am grateful to the participants at those meetings for their detailed comments. I am indebted to Pauline Wickham and Hannah Doe for their editorial advice. Several people found time in their busy schedules to comment on the draft manuscript and in particular I should like to thank Professor Michael Leifer of the London School of Economics, Dr Gerald Segal of the International Institute for Strategic Studies, Chris Sherwell of Smith New Court in London and Dr Carlyle Thayer of the Australian National University, who was also an excellent companion during a visit to Hanoi in November 1991. John Phipps provided valuable assistance with the chapter on 'Reform and the economy'. The map on the facing page is taken from William J. Duiker's *Vietnam Since the Fall of Saigon*, Ohio University Center for International Studies, Ohio, 1989, and is reproduced by kind permission of the publishers.

In Vietnam I should like to thank Nguyen Tuan Lieu, Director of the Institute of International Relations in Hanoi, and his colleagues for several hours of invaluable discussions. I am also grateful to Nguyen Co Thach, for many years Vietnamese foreign minister, and to officials of the foreign ministry for taking time to discuss their country's foreign policy. Professor Nguyen Thai Ninh of the Central Committee of the Communist Party was kind enough to debate his party's fortunes with a sceptical observer. Many in Vietnam will disagree with much of this study, but I hope it will be understood in the context of *doi moi*. For encouragement and moral support from New York and Strasbourg, thanks to Isobelle Jaques. And, finally, both the Royal Institute of International Affairs and I are extremely grateful to Enterprise Oil for financial support for this study.

May 1992   M.C.W.

1
INTRODUCTION

For most of the period since the end of the Second World War Vietnam has been at war with a daunting array of countries. The country's former foreign minister, Nguyen Co Thach, when asked once to comment on Vietnam's close relationship with the Soviet Union quipped that it was the only one of the five permanent members of the UN Security Council that his country had not engaged on the battlefield.[1] To the list of Britain, France, the United States and China could be added Japan and Democratic Kampuchea, as well as Australia and South Korea, both of whom committed substantial forces to fight alongside the United States in the 1960s. It is small wonder that the history of such prolonged conflict has seriously hampered Vietnam's economic and political development and has left it at the beginning of the 1990s with one of the few Marxist-Leninist regimes remaining in the world and its people with one of the lowest living standards in Asia.

In October 1991 nineteen foreign ministers and the Secretary-General of the United Nations gathered in Paris for a peace conference to settle the Cambodian conflict. The hope must be – for all parties to the Indochinese conflict – that, unlike the Geneva conference of 1954 or the Paris peace accords of 1973, the Paris conference of 1991 will bring lasting peace not only to Cambodia, but to Indochina as a whole. The very holding of the conference was testimony to the fact that Vietnam, having toppled the infamous Khmer Rouge from power in 1979, had finally realized that battlefield victories alone would never bring it the real independence and economic prosperity the country has so long desired. The signs are that the leadership in Hanoi has finally realized that only prolonged peace and a real engagement with the outside world will rescue the country from its current painful isolation and economic backwardness, and at the same time secure the continuing rule of the Communist Party. Recourse to arms is no longer an option.

As Vietnam entered the 1990s, it did so with few real friends in the world. Its once powerful patron, the former Soviet Union, had disintegrated, while all its former East European allies had decisively rejected communism. The process of rapprochement with China, on Peking's terms, was still in its initial stages. And, despite President Bush's proud claim in the wake of the Gulf war that the spectre of the Vietnam war had been buried forever, normalization of relations between Washington and Hanoi still seems a distant prospect. Washington's crippling economic embargo against Vietnam, denying virtually all lines of international credit, remains in place. Yet, despite this daunting international isolation, Vietnam's leaders have since the late 1980s committed themselves to wide-ranging economic reforms, desperately trying to bring Vietnam into the modern age.

This will be no easy task. Not only has Vietnam to overcome the legacy of almost five decades of conflict and to catch up with neighbours that have long outpaced it economically, but it also has to do it with a political system that now seems singularly out of place with the world at the end of the twentieth century. Indeed the question has to be posed as to whether Vietnam's political structure, based on the Leninist model of democratic centralism, is capable of delivering the economic development that the country now so urgently needs. The opposition of Vietnam's ruling Communist Party to political pluralism has often been repeated. Political authoritarianism and economic development have not, however, been uncommon bedfellows in East Asia, and in recent years Vietnamese officials have referred favourably to countries like Singapore and South Korea as models for their country. But the question for Vietnam is, can a party which saw its task historically as building socialism be the political vehicle for the transition to a market economy?

A grafitti slogan in the Paris Metro proclaimed recently, 'Communism the longest road to capitalism!' Vietnam's leaders have, since the sixth party congress in December 1986, adopted as their goal the task of reforming the economy along market lines while at the same time retaining party rule. In this endeavour no communist-ruled society has so far been successful. Indeed the experience of Eastern Europe, even of reformist regimes like Hungary and Poland, and of the Soviet Union itself would seem to indicate that meaningful economic reform, necessitating as it does popular support, can be successful only once the Communist

Party has been dislodged from power. Even in China, the pace of economic reform, which ran so successfully in the 1980s, has been blighted since 1989 by the Tiananmen massacre and the crude attempts of the party to retain power at all costs. It is difficult not to conclude that the gigantic historical project launched by Lenin and the Bolsheviks in 1917, and until recently so passionately endorsed by Ho Chi Minh and the leadership of the Vietnamese Communist Party, has run its course.[2]

Nevertheless the Vietnamese Communist Party, which has ruled North Vietnam since 1954 and the whole country since 1975, is the only leadership the country currently has. Other political alternatives do not seem feasible at the present time. It is, however, interesting to note that dissidence on the fringes of the Communist Party itself does exist and is likely to grow with the pace of reform. The commitment of the party to economic reform since 1986, and especially since 1988, is genuine enough. Any visitor to Vietnam since those dates can testify to the enormous changes that have been wrought in the country's life, and particularly in the economy. Changes in foreign policy have been equally remarkable, especially the willingness to abandon the 'special relationship' with Cambodia, for which so many Vietnamese lives were shed and which condemned Vietnam for so many years to international isolation. Without the retreat from Cambodia, the Paris peace conference in October 1991 would not have been possible. Yet, for the most part, these changes have been imposed on Vietnam by the outside world, and it remains to be seen whether the Communist Party has the political dynamism to match meaningful economic reform.

Real though the changes that have occurred in Vietnam are, the West has moved far too slowly to welcome them. In this regard the United States, shadowed by Japan, stands out. More than two years after Vietnam withdrew its forces from Cambodia, and despite extensive cooperation with Washington on the MIA (Missing in Action) issue, the United States has made only tentative steps towards normalizing relations with Vietnam. The maintenance of the economic embargo, and the concomitant denial of credit and assistance from the international lending institutions, are so punishing as to be interpreted as a vendetta. The lifting of that embargo would not only have an almost immediate effect on Vietnam, but would also lock the country's economic future so tightly into the international economy as to make a retreat into the Stalinist policies of the past virtually impossible. The maintenance of the embargo, even more punishing now with the collapse of Soviet economic aid, not only hurts ordinary Vietnamese but also means that a return to old Stalinist

3

orthodoxies, a new political authoritarianism or a complete collapse of the present political system cannot be completely ruled out. Any of these possibilities could fuel social unrest in Vietnam, would be disastrous for Vietnam's neighbours and would lead to yet another exodus of boat-people.

It is with these grim realities that Vietnam's leadership currently grapples. The success, or otherwise, of their efforts is likely to have far-reaching consequences for Southeast Asia, China and Japan as well as the United States. It is with this reform process and its likely future course that this study is primarily concerned.

The history of any nation shapes its present and its future. For Vietnam in the 1990s, as in the nineteenth century, its relationship with China and its neighbours in Southeast Asia is critical. Domestic reform cannot be successful without good relations prevailing with these neighbours. The treatment in this study is thematic and necessarily involves a certain amount of overlap. Chapter 2 examines the evolution of Vietnam's conflict-ridden history until 1975, without which an understanding of its present problems and likely future course is, I believe, impossible. The extraordinary domination of most twentieth-century Vietnamese politics by the Communist Party, founded by Ho Chi Minh, and its current efforts to thwart the fate of so many of its fraternal ruling parties are the subject of Chapter 3. If the party is to be successful in these latter endeavours, the success of its economic reforms is pivotal; it is to these that I turn in Chapter 4. I hasten to add that I am not an economist and it is with economic policy, rather than with microeconomics, that I am primarily concerned. Chapter 5 looks at the country's foreign policy, which for so long after 1975 was based on its close alliance with the Soviet Union and its 'special relationship' with Laos and Cambodia. By 1992 these foundation stones of Vietnamese foreign policy had disappeared and Vietnam was trying to come to terms not only with the member states of the Association of Southeast Asian Nations (ASEAN) and the European Community, but also with former battlefield enemies, such as China and the United States. Finally, Chapter 6 returns again to look at the arbiter of Vietnam's political destiny for so long, the Communist Party, to examine what the future might hold for it.

2
THE HISTORICAL BACKGROUND: VIETNAM'S SEARCH FOR IDENTITY

The identity of many nations is forged in conflict and in the search for territory. Inevitably, nations have tended to define themselves in terms of their neighbours. From the earliest times when it is possible to speak of a Vietnamese nation, Vietnamese have found themselves at odds with their neighbours, the Chinese, Cambodians and Thai. As the famous French sociologist of Vietnam, Paul Mus, wrote, 'Vietnam did not just happen: she occupied her territory only at the price of incessant wars'.[1] In looking at the span of Vietnamese history, it is possible to see the one and a quarter centuries of French and American involvement (1858–1975) as no more than an interregnum in Vietnam's attempt to come to a *modus vivendi* with its neighbours. Even the refrains of past struggles in Vietnamese history find a curious echo in the present. One of the favourite intellectual themes of Emperor Minh Mang (1820–41) was 'decadent China and orthodox Vietnam', especially true, he felt, with a barbarian dynasty, the Manchus, in control.[2] At the end of the 1970s, the leaders of Vietnam's Communist Party would adopt an almost identical refrain when explaining to their people, and to the world, that it was China that had abandoned socialism and Vietnam that remained true to Marxism-Leninism.

For a thousand years, until AD 939, China ruled Vietnam, and for much of the next nine hundred years Vietnam's rulers were preoccupied with thwarting Chinese attempts to reimpose imperial hegemony. Not surprisingly, the earliest heroes in Vietnamese history are the fabled Trung sisters, who in AD 40–42 rose in revolt against the Chinese overlords. By the time the Ly dynasty established itself in the Red River delta of northern Vietnam (1010–1225), the outlines of Vietnamese identity were relatively clear. Thus at about the same time that England and France were congealing into nation-states, so too was Vietnam. The political system was much more decentralized than in China, and Buddhism was already widespread. Above all, early Vietnamese society was far more militaristic than that of imperial China, a fact which enabled it to defeat the Mongol invaders in the thirteenth century who had raised such havoc in Europe. The invasion also produced Vietnam's first great military strategist, Tran Hung Dao. The celebration of these national heroes in Vietnamese folklore is evidence of a pride in pursuing a political destiny separate from that of China. As David Marr notes, 'For all the supposed impact of a millennium of Chinese rule, Ly society in Vietnam strikes the observer as essentially non-Confucian.'[3]

When they needed to, however, the Vietnamese adapted to Confucianism and Chinese ways, either to please the imperial rulers in Peking or for their own benefit. Thus during the Le dynasty (1428–1788), Chinese systems and concepts were more systematically adopted, aiding the Vietnamese greatly in their thrust to the south. It gave them the political apparatus and the tax base to crush the Hindu kingdom of Champa in central Vietnam in 1470–71 and then to start their equally relentless push south against the Khmer or Cambodians. But while the Vietnamese scholar-gentry of the period were profoundly conscious of their cultural, intellectual and moral debt to China and to Chinese models, the people, by contrast, were all too aware of the differences in language, costume and general physical bearing that separated them from the Chinese. Thus was born an elite/mass dichotomy that was to replicate itself in the twentieth century when Vietnamese elites adopted French and later American ways.

During the Nguyen dynasty, founded by Emperor Gia Long in 1802, Vietnam witnessed a substantial reassertion of Confucian values and institutions. The Confucian state in Vietnam on the eve of European intervention was authoritarian, but retained a ritualistic preserve between itself and its subjects. It intervened in rural life, but more as a coordinator than as an executive. Responsibility for implementation of imperial directives remained with the village. At the same time the domain presided over by the Nguyen rulers extended by the early nineteenth century over most of what we now know as Vietnam. Expansion south into the Mekong delta had brought Vietnam into conflict with Cambodia, over which it vied for influence with Thailand. Had it not been for French intervention, the Cambodian kingdom might have been gradually taken over by Vietnam as had the kingdom of Champa earlier, a possibility that was to have a powerful resonance when the Khmer Rouge were to hold political power in Cambodia in the late 1970s.

But while Vietnam's population was much larger than that of Cambodia, and its political and military structure much more sophisticated, like most Asian nations in the mid-nineteenth century it was unable to withstand the superior technology of European arms. Nevertheless, unlike other Southeast Asian countries which had earlier succumbed to European intervention, such as the Philippines, Indonesia and Malaya, Vietnam was already a clearly defined nation-state. In Vietnam, as the French were to learn, an established pre-colonial tradition existed, a well-formed culture and language, and an effective political and economic system. As Huynh Kim Khanh writes, in confronting French colonial power, 'the Vietnamese national movement resembled the classic nationalism of Europe rather than most former colonial possessions in Asia and Africa'.[4]

The arrival of the French

In September 1858, French naval forces landed at Da Nang, where just over a century later, in March 1965, the first American marines landed. So began almost a century of French colonial rule that was to last until France's ignominious defeat at Dien Bien Phu in 1954. Although it was not until 1885 that French rule extended over all of what is now Vietnam, in the following decades the country's social structure and economy were to be fundamentally altered. The powers of the monarchy, and of the traditional scholar-gentry through which they ruled, were gradually but irrevocably eroded.[5] Although resistance to French rule continued for many years to come, Vietnam became divided as never before. The traditional ruling order was coopted to serve French colonial rule. Already by 1900 the authority of Confucian ideology and social institutions, and of the scholar-gentry that had defended the old social order, was rapidly dissipating. Ironically, it was from the ranks of sons of the scholar-gentry that the early communists were to find many of their most promising recruits. By the early twentieth century many Vietnamese in the cities and towns already took French rule for granted. In the countryside it was a different matter, and tax protests such as those that swept central Vietnam in 1908 were quite common.[6] But in effect the traditional Vietnamese state had already ceased to exist, replaced by a new colonial state, which for good measure even took a new capital, abandoning the imperial city of Hué for Hanoi.

Vietnam's colonization intensified the strictly provincial differences separating the South from the centre or the North. The Mekong delta region of the South, or Cochinchina as the French called it, is among the richest rice lands in Southeast Asia, whereas the centre, Annam, is little more than a narrow strip of land where the mountains almost come down to the sea, and the North, Tonkin, although another delta region, affords the peasants little more than a subsistence living from the land. Tonkin was so close to the subsistence level that it often had to import rice from Cochinchina, a practice that has remained until the present day. Despite its economic backwardness, however, Tonkin's capital, Hanoi, was the seat of the French Governor-General of Indochina.

If Hanoi was the administrative centre for French rule in Vietnam, the southern city of Saigon was the country's commercial centre. It was in Saigon and its environs that commercial development took place. Especially after the First World War, it was here that capital development was concentrated, focusing mainly on agriculture as an export industry. Rubber was the primary commodity, with the acreage used for its cultivation tripling between 1917 and 1926. Rice exports also expanded considerably, with a capacity of exporting two million tons of rice annually, a figure Vietnam was not able to match even with the economic reforms of the late 1980s. Most of the economic development of the region, however, was in the hands not of a thrusting bourgeoisie but of either *colon* settlers or Chinese. Indeed, contrary to the analyses of Vietnamese Marxists later, Vietnam never did develop a viable independent bourgeois class. Local industries as such were discouraged in favour of imports from metropolitan France.

In this respect colonial economic development in Vietnam was not very different from that in British Burma or the Dutch East Indies. Those few Vietnamese who were to rise to the meteoric heights of the new bourgeoisie tended almost without exception to be subordinates or adjuncts of the dominant French capitalists and administrators. Without substantial economic independence, they tended also to be politically immature. Their position is summed up by Marr: 'Of all Vietnamese social classes in the twentieth century, the bourgeoisie had the weakest sense of economic identity.'[7]

But it was not only in the towns and cities or the capitalist Mekong delta region that Vietnamese life was transformed. In the countryside, too, the past rural equilibrium, and above all the sense of community, was ruptured by the new French colonial order. Commercialization brought with it growing social stratification. The framework of village life was struck a body blow by the French concept of taxes, payable in money and on an individual basis and levied on a scale that seemed exorbitant to the peasant. The effect on village life was far-reaching. As Paul Mus notes, one of the most astute observers of Vietnamese society:

> The traditional village could not survive. It continued to look the same, at least in Tonkin and in Annam, but it became an empty shell, void of the social substance it had once had which had kept life constantly renewed. With the heart gone out of it, even the appearance of the village was in a precarious position unless there could be a complete reversal in direction, back to the lost equilibrium of life.[8]

Thus the Confucian balance that had existed between the ritualistic state and the autarchic village was brought to ruin, without anything to replace it. In many respects the effect of colonial rule in Vietnam was not very different from the fate that peasantries suffered elsewhere in Southeast Asia. What was to separate Vietnam from its neighbours was the intervention of a revolutionary party that was able to sink deep roots into the countryside in an effort to restore the lost equilibrium. Already in 1930 the potentialities of the Communist Party were demonstrated in widespread rural revolts in the central Vietnamese provinces of Nghe-An and Ha Tinh.[9] As we shall see later, it was the communists who were to prove the most capable and adept champions of a new vision of a Vietnamese community. Thus since the Second World War the Vietnamese have been waging a struggle not only over the form of their state, but over the nature of Vietnamese society, the very identity of the Vietnamese.

As in other Southeast Asian societies, the Second World War brought profound change to Vietnam. The capitulation of France to Nazi Germany in June 1940 had been totally unexpected in Indochina, where French military prowess and invincibility had appeared to be a permanent fact of life. The declining power of the French was further underlined to the Vietnamese by the agreement reached between Vichy France and Japan in September 1940 allowing Japanese troops to be based in Vietnam in return for recognition of French sovereignty over Indochina. The war brought with it increasing hardships for the population. Unemployment rose markedly as economic activity, especially in the export sector, ground to a halt. Taxes and war requisitions became punitive, and by 1943 government seizure of paddy rice had begun to cause serious unrest in the countryside. By the winter of 1944–5, famine had struck.

But quite apart from the dire economic predicament of the Vietnamese people during these years, it was the political situation which had changed irrevocably. Ironically, the failure of the Japanese to impose direct imperial rule over Vietnam, as they did for example in Burma or Indonesia, had two important consequences for Vietnam. In the first place it meant that a nationalist movement under Japanese tutelage did not come about in Vietnam, as it did in Burma under Aung San or in Indonesia under Sukarno. Thus in the postwar period the Vietnamese communists did not have to contend for power with powerful nationalist movements, as did their counterparts in Burma and Indonesia. Secondly, the preservation of French rule by the Japanese, in what amounted to no more than a client role, further eroded the legitimacy of French sovereignty. In March 1945, sensing their declining position in the wider Pacific war, the Japanese staged a coup against the French, abolishing the colonial administration and interning its military forces. In a few hours, eighty years of French rule was brought to an end. On 11 March, Tokyo declared Vietnam's independence under Japanese tutelage, but chose as its leader not a prominent nationalist like Aung San or Sukarno, but the Emperor Bao Dai, a figurehead with no real political constituency. Highly conscious of his own weak position as puppet of the fading power of Japan, Bao Dai was within a few months to abdicate and request the communist Viet Minh to form a government. As Paul Mus noted, France had lost title to the Confucian Heavenly Mandate by its failure to protect the Vietnamese from the Japanese. Political legitimacy would be granted to whatever force could effectively claim power and re-establish order. In the vacuum created by the Japanese surrender to the Allies in August 1945, there were no real contenders for power other than Ho Chi Minh's communist forces.

The Thirty Years War
The proclamation of independence on 2 September 1945 by Ho Chi Minh, founder of the Democratic Republic of Vietnam (DRV), was not, however, to go uncontested. Indeed, Ho was never to see fulfilled in his lifetime his dream of a unified, independent Vietnam. The independence declaration in September 1945 was to prove merely the harbinger of three decades of almost unbroken war, which claimed the lives of millions of Vietnamese and tens of thousands of Frenchmen and Americans. Probably no other nation in the post-1945 world has experienced such prolonged and bitter conflict as Vietnam. Its legacy is all too evident today.

The war started almost immediately. In Saigon the hold of the revolutionary Viet Minh forces over the city was contested by British and French forces. France, like the Netherlands in Indonesia in 1945, was determined to try to reimpose European colonial rule. Initially, however, the French position was weak politically and militarily, with France itself only just beginning to recover from the ravages of German occupation. In March 1946 France even recognized the legitimacy of the Vietnamese republic within the context of the French Union. Peace negotiations were held in 1946 in Dalat and Fontainebleau. The negotiations faltered, however, with France, like the Netherlands in Indonesia, failing to recognize the dramatically changed circumstances in Southeast Asia after the Second World War. Both colonial powers were essentially unwilling to grant the substance of independence.

In December 1946 full-scale war broke out between the Viet Minh and the French expeditionary forces. The first Indochina war had begun in earnest, one of the most bitter and prolonged in the history of decolonization. The war turned into a civil war two years later, when Bao Dai was chosen once again by the occupying power to head a nominally independent government. His government had all the trappings and attributes of legality, but it was seen by the vast majority of the Vietnamese people as a French creation. It was not a difficult task for Ho and the Viet Minh to portray themselves as the only true representatives of the spirit of resistance against foreign rule. The war continued unabated and effectively became internationalized in 1950. With the triumph of the communists under Mao Zedong in China and the outbreak of war in Korea, France sought to portray the war in Vietnam as part of the general fight against communism in East Asia and not as a struggle for independence. Fatefully, after the visit to Washington in September 1951 of General Lattre de Tassigny, the United States accepted this premise. American military aid, which had started in May 1950, was by 1953 funding 80% of the war. Increasingly, the United States was drawn into the conflict, sending military advisory teams to Vietnam and effectively bankrolling the French war effort. This was already the era of Graham Greene's *Quiet American*.

In Vietnam itself the war developed a new intensity, with the Viet Minh, under the command of General Vo Nguyen Giap, increasingly availing themselves of substantial quantities of Chinese weaponry. With the death of Stalin and the end of the Korean war in 1953, the international climate changed and efforts to find a diplomatic solution intensified. On 7 May 1954 an international conference on Indochina was convened in

Geneva, chaired by Great Britain and the Soviet Union. On the very day, however, that the conference opened, the strategic French fortress at Dien Bien Phu surrendered to General Giap's forces. It was a bitter and humiliating blow for the French and spelled the end of France as a power in Indochina. Its dénouement gave the Vietnamese immense self-confidence in their battle prowess. The extraordinary feat of the Viet Minh forces seemed to confirm for the communist leadership the importance of fighting and negotiating to obtain their political goals. Their victory at Dien Bien Phu, even at the cost of substantial losses of their own forces, underlined that recourse to arms was always an option.[10]

The Geneva conference ended on 21 July with agreement on the division of Vietnam at the seventeenth parallel, even though the Viet Minh were estimated to control three quarters of Vietnam.[11] Thus, Vietnam joined the ranks of those other nations divided by the cold war, Germany and Korea. For the first time, Vietnam's communist leadership realized that its allies, the Soviet Union and China, were quite willing to sacrifice Vietnamese interests for their own wider diplomatic purposes. The armistice agreement and final declaration also called for elections to assure the unification of the country by July 1956. What was to become known as 'the Geneva Agreement of 1954' was in fact a series of armistice agreements between the French army and the Viet Minh. Nothing else was signed, particularly not the final declaration made at the conference. The pro-western government in southern Vietnam did not seek to hide its disagreement with the final declaration.

From the beginning, the omens for the agreement reached at Geneva were not good. Although the legitimacy of the DRV, at least in North Vietnam, was recognized, the communists were very reluctant to withdraw their forces from southern Vietnam. France made it clear that its interest in future political cooperation extended only to South Vietnam, thus leaving the communist North little other choice than to rely on China and the Soviet Union. Moreover, the day after the conference President Eisenhower announced the start of negotiations which were to lead to the signing in Manila in September of the Southeast Asia Collective Defence Treaty, creating SEATO, emphasizing further the isolation of the DRV and the continuation of the cold war in the region. Thus was lost another opportunity by the West to cooperate with Vietnam's communist government. In this atmosphere the new government in Saigon, led by Ngo Dinh Diem, felt no compunction about violating the provisions of the Geneva agreement. Within months a wave of repression was launched against Viet Minh supporters in South Vietnam, and Diem steadfastly refused to hold the proposed 1956 referendum on unification.

The communist regime in North Vietnam, led by Ho Chi Minh, regarded the government of South Vietnam as little more than an American puppet regime. Eight out of fourteen ministers in Diem's government had served in French sponsored administrations, and virtually all the senior South Vietnamese military officers had fought alongside the French.[12] In the view of the party leadership in Hanoi, the United States had simply replaced France as the imperialist enemy.

After a brief hiatus, the communists in Vietnam resumed the revolutionary struggle in the South with the founding, in 1960, of the National Liberation Front (NLF), a classic communist united front organization. Its revolutionary struggle included a campaign of assassination of local government officials. Escalation of the war against the regime of Ngo Dinh Diem increasingly brought the communist forces into conflict with the United States, whose involvement in Vietnam deepened after the assassination of Diem in 1963, against a background of growing Buddhist agitation against the regime. At the same time the war in South Vietnam moved from being an internal conflict between communist and anti-communist forces to a full-scale war between North Vietnam and the United States. In August 1964, on the pretext of a North Vietnamese attack on US naval craft (the so-called Tonkin Gulf incident), President Lyndon B. Johnson ordered the first air attacks on North Vietnam.[13] In March the following year the first regular US combat units arrived in Da Nang and the air war over North Vietnam had begun. By the summer of 1965 US forces were involved in serious fighting in the Central Highlands and along the coast. Although heavy casualties were inflicted on the NLF and North Vietnamese forces, the response of the communist leaders in Hanoi was to send further reinforcements south. Their resolve to do so was fortified by massive US bombing of North Vietnam, which in the next three years had more bombs dropped on it than were used throughout the Second World War.

From this time on, it was US forces that bore the brunt of some of the heaviest fighting in the South. The United States had become involved militarily not only to strengthen the South Vietnamese regime, from 1967 led by General Nguyen Van Thieu, but also to demonstrate to the communist leadership in Hanoi, and aspiring communist insurgencies elsewhere, the US resolve to prevent successful 'national liberation' struggles. At the same time American policymakers saw their involvement as part of their strategy to contain the Soviet Union and China. But

13

the United States seriously underestimated the extent to which the communist movement and nationalism in Vietnam were almost synonymous. And the more the US became involved in propping up successive South Vietnamese regimes, the more the communists were able to appeal successfully to Vietnamese nationalism. In addition, US strategy, because it concentrated on the physical control of population and territory, ignored the main source of support for the NLF, namely the peasantry. Local studies of the war confirm the NLF's almost constant support among the peasantry.[14]

Increasingly, the dominant theme of the war in Vietnam appeared to be not a civil war between communists and non-communists, but a war between the United States and the Vietnamese communists, given substantial military and economic assistance by the Soviet Union and China, with the South Vietnamese government playing a marginal role. Without doubt this was the perception of most Vietnamese in the South, especially in the countryside. And as in the earlier struggle against the French, the Vietnamese communists successfully adopted the nationalist mantle. To more and more South Vietnamese their government seemed little more than a puppet regime.

The end of the war

More than any other conflict after the Second World War, the war in Vietnam seemed to symbolize the struggle of Third World radical nationalism against the determination of the United States to stem the tide of communism in the developing world. Ironically, the massive involvement of the United States in the conflict in Vietnam merely postponed an almost inevitable communist victory and succeeded in contributing to the eventual communist successes in Laos and Cambodia as well.

In late January 1968, communist forces launched a sustained offensive throughout South Vietnam to coincide with the annual New Year's festival or Tet. The most prominent attacks were on Saigon itself and the former imperial capital, Hué. While the losses of the communist forces during the offensive were considerable, the psychological damage inflicted on the United States through the extensive television coverage amounted to a political victory for Hanoi. In Saigon, parts of the US embassy itself were briefly occupied, while in Hué the NLF and North Vietnamese forces succeeded in holding parts of the city for three weeks. Despite the fact that the offensive had not led to a popular general uprising in Saigon, as the communists had hoped for in a repeat of the

August 1945 uprising, the North Vietnamese and their NLF allies proved far more capable of sustaining the losses of the campaign than did the Americans or the Saigon regime.

The Tet offensive was a dramatic turning-point in the Vietnam war. It became apparent to the Johnson administration in Washington that despite the commitment of 500,000 troops the war could not be won militarily. Within months of the offensive, President Johnson had suspended the bombing of North Vietnam and opened peace talks in Paris. He also announced that he would not be seeking another term of office. Fighting continued while the Paris talks dragged on, but on a smaller scale if only because of the heavy casualties both sides suffered during the Tet offensive. Under Richard Nixon, who assumed the US presidency in January 1969, the United States pursued a policy of 'Vietnamization' of the war, withdrawing some troops and increasingly leaving most counter-insurgency operations to South Vietnamese forces. The last major offensive operation involving US forces was the April 1970 invasion of Cambodia, which succeeded only in contributing to the rise of the Khmer Rouge and alienating even larger numbers of American people from the war in Indochina.

After more than four years of talks in Paris, North Vietnam and the United States finally signed an agreement on 23 January 1973 providing for the complete withdrawal of American forces, a cease-fire between South Vietnamese and communist forces, and the formation of an ill-defined national council for reconciliation in the South. By the end of March the last American combat troops had been withdrawn and American assistance to the South Vietnamese government sharply curtailed. But, as with the Geneva Agreement some nineteen years earlier, peace was not restored to Vietnam. In the weeks and months following the cease-fire, negotiations on a future political structure and on a military settlement quickly broke down amid mutual recriminations. Soon communist and South Vietnamese forces were fighting again.

Expectations in Hanoi had been high after the Paris Peace Accords that the Thieu regime could be overthrown without resort to further armed force. The South Vietnamese government, however, remained unwilling to see the NLF, since 1969 known as the Provisional Revolutionary Government, accommodated in the political structure of the southern half of Vietnam. Moreover, the revolutionary forces were not strong enough by themselves to engineer Thieu's downfall. In these circumstances, in the autumn of 1974 the communist leadership in Hanoi decided to launch a major offensive in the South in early 1975.

Subsequent accounts by Vietnamese leaders make it clear that the success of the 1975 offensive and the quick demise of the Thieu regime exceeded all expectations in Hanoi.[15] In the first stage of the offensive, in January, communist forces captured Phuoc Long province, northeast of Saigon. Two months later, they seized Ban Me Thuot, the largest city in the Central Highlands, with very little resistance. President Thieu made the fatal mistake of ordering a retreat from the northern part of the country, leaving only the coastal cities defended. Panic now beset the South Vietnamese army, and by the end of March Hué, the former imperial capital, was in communist hands.

It was at this stage that the Politburo in Hanoi, flushed with the continuing success of the offensive and convinced that the United States would not intervene to save the beleaguered Thieu regime, decided to press for final victory. Communist forces poured south from the Central Highlands and along the coast, and by mid-April were on the outskirts of Saigon. For a brief period they were halted by stiff resistance from South Vietnamese troops at Xuan Loc, less than 100 kilometers east of Saigon. By 21 April, thirteen North Vietnamese divisions had surrounded the South Vietnamese capital. The following day, General Thieu resigned and left the country. The presidency was taken over by General Duong Van Minh, who vainly sought a negotiated settlement with the communists. But on April 30, with South Vietnamese resistance at an end, and helicopters evacuating the remaining Americans from rooftops, North Vietnamese troops stormed into the grounds of the presidential palace in Saigon. The second Indochina war had come to an end.

In retrospect, it is difficult to see how the Americans could have won the war in Vietnam. The obstacles facing the United States when it intervened decisively in 1965 were already insurmountable. The South Vietnamese government was inefficient and corrupt, lacked legitimacy among the peasantry and was regarded as little more than a continuation of the old French colonial regime. By contrast, the communist-led NLF offered a forceful and convincing vision of an alternative future. No matter how dreadful the losses suffered by the communists in battle, there was no shortage of volunteers to come forward and replace the diminished ranks. Grim tenacity marked every step of the Vietnamese war effort.[16]

For the young and the idealistic, the communists offered the vision of a unified socialist Vietnam that would take a place of honour among the nations of the world struggling against western imperialism. The revolution also offered an avenue of social advancement more exciting than anything the Saigon regime could offer. While the more astute American observers, such as John Paul Vann, were well aware of the alienation of the peasantry from the South Vietnamese government, what they continually underestimated was the appeal of the communists to the most politically aware segment of the countryside.[17] This appeal, combined with the ruthlessness with which the NLF and their North Vietnamese allies conducted the war, rendered America's war effort vain, no matter how sophisticated or how many troops were deployed to counter the enemy. Despite intense effort and great dedication, not to mention the loss of life and funds, any American hope of 'harnessing the revolution' and making a weak society strong was doomed in the absence of a viable and substantive South Vietnamese political ally. More than any other communist movement, the Vietnamese communists had succeeded in identifying the modern identity of the state with their struggle.

3

THE POLITICAL BACKGROUND: VIETNAMESE COMMUNISM

When the Vietnamese Communist Party held its fourth congress in December 1976, the first following the reunification of the country, 214 of the 1,008 delegates attending the conference had been active in the party ranks before the August revolution of 1945. Of these, 25 had been anticolonial activists in the 1920s, and remained prominent leaders of the party well into the 1980s.[1] They included the party General Secretary Le Duan, Truong Chinh, who succeeded him in June 1986, and Prime Minister Pham Van Dong, who retained that post until June 1987 and who still acts as an adviser to the party Politburo. The continued prominence of these men in the party leadership well into the 1980s is striking testimony to the continuity in revolutionary leadership in Vietnam.

The party they led in the 1980s was the third largest communist party in the world, eclipsed in size only by the Soviet and Chinese communist parties. With the exception of North Korea, it was the only party that had come to power in Asia at the end of the Second World War and, unlike North Korea, had done so entirely through its own efforts. It was also the only communist party that had come to power in two stages: in 1945–54 in the North and in 1975 in the South. Indeed, within the pantheon of world communism, until the movement's sudden collapse in the late 1980s, the Vietnamese party has always felt that it occupied a unique place.

In part this stemmed from the stature of its first leader, Ho Chi Minh, who, while not an original theoretician, was one of the most successful communist revolutionaries, but more importantly from the party's perceived role in defeating first France and then the United States on the battlefield. Because of this, until very recently, Vietnam's party leaders have felt that their experiences had validity far outside the borders of their country and have placed great emphasis on their membership of what was latterly called the socialist commonwealth.[2]

Communism has undoubtedly achieved remarkable political success in Vietnam. Against herculean odds, a communist cell of nine men in 1925 had grown by December 1976 into a mass party of one and a half million and had come to power having defeated militarily two of the strongest powers in the world. Indeed, tragically for Vietnam, it was the very success of the communists as revolutionaries and as fighters that proved to be one of the main reasons for Vietnam's failure to adjust to the more mundane tasks of national development after the end of the war in 1975.

The Vietnamese Communist Party was founded by Ho Chi Minh in February 1930 in Hong Kong.[3] The party was a fusion of existing revolutionary groups, its main component being the Thanh Nien (Revolutionary Youth) association, which had been formed in 1925. The party's formation came at about the same time as the founding of communist parties in the Philippines and Malaya, and some sixteen years after the founding of the first Marxist groups in Indonesia. Yet, with the exception of the Chinese Communist Party, the Vietnamese has enjoyed greater political success than any other Asian party. In large part this success can be attributed to its ability from early days to identify itself with Vietnamese nationalism, and to harness that nationalism to the cause of a wider international revolutionary struggle. In embracing communism in the interwar period, Ho Chi Minh and other Vietnamese intellectuals saw in the ideology a means not only to attain their country's independence, but also to revitalize and modernize Vietnamese society.[4] When this message was interpreted for the peasantry there is little doubt that it had considerable millenarian appeal.

It also has to be said that in Vietnamese society, unlike other Asian societies, communism has had no other ideology to contend with. By the 1930s the traditional Confucian value system was already thoroughly discredited. And no other nationalist parties of substance developed in Vietnam to contest the Communist Party's domination of the movement against first the French and then the Americans. From the very beginning in 1925 the communist movement has always dominated the Vietnamese political stage. The absence of countervailing ideologies – such as Catholicism in the Philippines, or Islam in Malaysia and Indonesia – or of institutions such as the monarchy in Thailand has made the communists' task that much easier. Non-communist parties faced an almost hopeless situation. Those nationalist parties that appeared were more factions than parties, revolving around an individual or based on regional or ethnic identities. As William Duiker has noted:

> Part of the problem appeared to be that the erosion of the traditional
> bonds of Confucianism had cut many of the emotional ties linking
> urban intellectuals with the mass of the rural population. Unlike
> many other colonial societies in South and Southeast Asia, where
> activist intellectuals were able to call on the common bond of a
> great traditional religion – Hinduism, Buddhism, or Islam – and to
> knit together an anticolonial alliance throughout urban and rural
> areas of colonial society ... In Vietnam such an ideology did not exist.[5]

Thus one looks in vain for a Vietnamese equivalent of the Indian
Congress Party, or of UMNO in Malaysia, or the Nationalist Party of
Sukarno (PNI) in Indonesia. In the interwar period, the communists had
already monopolized opposition to the colonial power. And in the Japanese interregnum, as we have seen earlier, in contrast to its policy elsewhere in Southeast Asia, Tokyo gave limited encouragement to Vietnamese nationalism. After 1945, not only were other political parties never free
from the stigma of collaborating with the French or the Americans, but they
had to contend with the fact that the creation of the first modern Vietnamese state, the Democratic Republic of Vietnam, was effectively a political accomplishment of the Communist Party. The first non-communist
government that came to power did so not as a result of its own efforts,
but because it was imposed from above by the French. All the Saigon
governments after the Geneva conference bore the imprint of that hallmark.
Needless to say, since assuming full power in North Vietnam in 1954 and
throughout the country since 1975, the party has ascribed fully to the
Leninist party's traditional monopoly of political power.

In its first forty-five years of existence the Communist Party held only
three congresses, in 1935, 1951 and 1960.[6] That fact in itself emphasizes
that the primary task of the party throughout that period was the prosecu-
tion of revolutionary war. Indeed, even the fourth party congress, held in
December 1976, was to be the prelude to war with Cambodia (Democratic Kampuchea) and China. Only in the 1980s were party congresses
to meet in peacetime.

Vietnam at unification
The communist seizure of power in South Vietnam in April 1975 represents one of the great revolutionary triumphs of modern times. But the

nature of that triumph was to have fateful consequences for post-revolutionary Vietnam. The victory in 1975 was essentially a triumph of revolutionary organization and military strategy, rather than a spontaneous popular uprising. After decades of war, little else could probably have been expected. There was nothing comparable with the popular character of the August revolution of 1945, or even with the Tet uprising of 1968, when at least most of the fighting was done by local revolutionary forces, the National Liberation Front or Vietcong. By contrast, in 1975, not only was there little popular enthusiasm for the communist victory, but that victory itself had been achieved for the main part by regular units of the North Vietnamese Army. Even as sympathetic an observer as Khanh concedes that when they entered Saigon, the North Vietnamese forces met 'a bewildered, battered population that, long imbued with anti-communist propaganda, was both relieved by the coming of peace and uncertain about its fate under the victors'.[7]

Except in a few neighbourhoods, the entry of the revolutionary army into Saigon was met with silence, if not sullenness.[8] There were strong reasons for the absence of popular support for the revolutionary forces. Principal among them was the sheer war-weariness of a populace that had known almost relentless war since 1945. Moreover, the revolutionary forces in the South had suffered an appalling rate of attrition during the Tet offensive and as a result of the notorious Phoenix programme.[*] According to US military sources, during the Tet attacks alone the revolutionary forces had lost 32,000 dead.[9] Communist Party membership in the South was also comparatively small. In 1976 there were only 200,000 members out of a total national membership of 1,500,000. If force of arms brought about the final victory, it was the regular forces of the North Vietnamese army who were responsible and not local revolutionary forces.

Very few of the leadership in Hanoi had recent experience of the South and all were opposed to any idea of a specific southern regional identity. But especially in the cities a decade of strong American influence, which at its height included 500,000 US troops, had dramatically changed southern society. In essence, the cities had become a service economy for the American war effort. Countless thousands were employed by US bases and offices, while an even larger number serviced the every need of the American soldier. The consumer needs of this

---

*The Phoenix programme was a sophisticated counter-intelligence campaign designed to eliminate the NLF local leadership by capture or by encouraging them to defect, or even, in many cases, by physical liquidation.

society were met by imports, which were financed by US economic assistance. The departure of the Americans and the removal of their substantial buying power created severe economic and psychological withdrawal problems for the urban economy, and especially Saigon. It is not difficult to see in this the origins of the 'boat-people' problem. The party leadership was well aware of all this and was also conscious of its failure to build a real urban revolutionary base outside of a small group of party militants. It was this realization which had compelled it from the late 1960s to adopt a more military approach than it had done hitherto.

The triumph of that military approach, remarkable though it was in terms of courage and tenacity, was not a promising start on which to build a new society. For sure, the unity and independence of the Vietnamese people had been achieved for the first time since 1858. But it was an administrative unity imposed as a consequence of military victory. Undoubtedly, the nature of that victory, and the leadership's worries about southern society, propelled Hanoi to move quickly to dispel any idea of southern autonomy. There was no meaningful resistance from the remnants of the *ancien régime*, but political power had to be consolidated. Re-education camps were set up for the internment of tens of thousands of soldiers and civil servants of the former South Vietnamese government.[10] And despite the 1973 Paris Peace Agreements, which called for the establishment of a three-party Council for National Reconciliation in southern Vietnam, the last vestiges of autonomy in the South were quickly stripped away.[11] In April 1976, elections were held for a new National Assembly, and on 2 July the two halves of the country were formally united, adopting the name Socialist Republic of Vietnam.

Forward to socialism
In the wake of the collapse of communism in Eastern Europe, and in the Soviet Union itself, it is easier than ever to see the roots of the failure in Leninism. A revolutionary doctrine shaped at the beginning of the twentieth century to capture the state had proved singularly ill adapted by the end of the twentieth century to cope with the exigencies of the modern international economy or to provide for the most basic needs and aspirations of the peoples in whose name it ruled. The victory of the Vietnamese communists in 1975 may well in retrospect be seen as the last triumph of Bolshevism. That victory occurred some forty-five years after the founding of the party by Ho Chi Minh in Hong Kong in 1930. The whole of that period had seen an unremitting revolutionary struggle

before the goal of a unified state had been achieved, giving the Vietnamese communists a longer experience of revolution than any other ruling party. Even though the communist victory had been complete in the North by 1954, the construction of socialism was inevitably limited by military constraints, especially after the start of the US air war in 1965. After the decades of struggle, it is understandable if, after 1975, the Communist Party seemed in a rush to implement socialism. Moreover, as the leadership began to realize the full scope of problems facing it in the South, so the answer seemed to lie in tighter government control of the wayward southerners.[12]

Unification in 1976 coincided with the launching of a second five-year plan, the first having run in the North from 1961 to 1965. In the same year the ruling party significantly changed its name from the Vietnam Workers' Party (Lao Dong) to the Vietnamese Communist Party, symbolizing its new determination to step ahead with a socialist agenda. In December 1976 the party held what was only the fourth congress in its history, proclaiming the completion of the 'national' mission and the beginning of socialist construction throughout Vietnam. Despite the problems already evident in the South, and the urgent need to embark on economic reconstruction, the mood of the conference was triumphalist. And with victory still fresh in the leadership's mind, the way forward was seen in terms of rigorous communist orthodoxy. Socialist transformation of the South was to be complete by 1980. With unification complete, it was argued, it was now necessary to emphasize the proletarian and vanguard character of the party, in contrast to the earlier period of the struggle for national unification and independence, when patriotism was put in the foreground and concessions made to petit-bourgeois interests.[13]

The party leadership that emerged from the 1976 congress was essentially the same as that which presided over the last congress in 1960. Only three members of the 1960 Politburo were not included: two (including Ho Chi Minh) because they had died, and one, Hoang Van Hoan, because, as was later to become obvious, of differences with the party leader, Le Duan. Indeed, most of the leading members of the Politburo had been in the party leadership since the early 1940s. According to one estimate, as late as the seventh party congress in 1991, only thirty individuals had served on the party Politburo in its more than sixty-year history.[14] While their presence emphasized a continuity and cohesion in revolutionary leadership, their hold on power well into the 1980s led to an atrophy and paralysis of the Vietnamese body politic. Their lifetime experience of struggle caused them again and again to opt for the revolutionary solution, which, domestically, meant subscribing to traditional Leninist norms and dealing out harsh punishment for those opposed to the party, and externally meant continued recourse to arms.

The other striking feature that emerges in studying the leadership of the Vietnamese Communist Party is the absence in its history of anything resembling the personality cults around Stalin or Mao Zedong. Ho Chi Minh always abjured any such practice in the Vietnamese leadership and instead stressed collective leadership.[15] After his death in 1969, no one individual inherited the mantle of authority. Le Duan, who was General Secretary of the party for more than a quarter of a century (from 1960 until his death in July 1986), never enjoyed the pre-eminent role in the party that Ho did, although he is sometimes seen today in Vietnam as the country's Brezhnev.

But while collective leadership is preferable to the cults that have surrounded some Asian communist leaders, such as Mao Zedong and Kim Il Sung, it has led in the case of Vietnam to an unwillingness to take decisive action to address the nation's problems. A painfully slow process of consensus is needed before action can be taken; moreover, because government is subservient to the ruling party, its room for manoeuvre has been severely constrained. Collective leadership has brought with it a constant necessity to compromise in order to maintain balance on the Politburo. Thus, during the 1950s and 1960s, a balance had to be maintained between those who wished to prosecute the war in the South and those who wanted to build socialism in the North; in the 1960s and 1970s, between those who tilted towards the Soviet Union and those who tilted towards China; and in the 1980s, between those who enthusiastically embraced economic reform and those who favoured political conservativism. By and large, this precarious balancing-act has been maintained. Its most notable breakdown was in the late 1970s, when Vietnam aligned itself with the Soviet Union, prompting the only major split in the party in the post-1945 era and the dramatic defection to China of Hoang Van Hoan.[16]

Even more remarkable than maintaining this balance for decades has been the essentially unchanged composition of the leadership group. The key figures in this group were Le Duan, Truong Chinh, Le Duc Tho, Pham Van Dong, Vo Nguyen Giap, Pham Hung, Nguyen Van Linh, Van Tien Dung and Mai Chi Tho. All were to hold on to their leadership posts well into their late seventies and in some cases into their eighties. Indeed, one of the major features of Vietnam's political crisis in the 1980s was the continuance in power of this rapidly ageing and ailing group. As in the Soviet Union in the Brezhnevite period, many leaders have died in office.

Prising power away from this ageing group of leaders has been a difficult and protracted task. Le Duan, who was General Secretary from 1960 until July 1986, held power for more than a quarter of a century, almost as long as Stalin's reign of power in the Soviet Union. Remarkably, he was succeeded by Truong Chinh, who had been General Secretary thirty years earlier. By the time of the sixth party congress in December 1986, both Truong Chinh and the Prime Minister, Pham Van Dong, were eighty years old. And although the sixth party congress took major steps in the direction of economic reform, and several leading Politburo members resigned, they were retained as advisers to the party central committee.

The sixth party congress: perestroika in Vietnam

Le Duan's death in July 1986 began the painfully slow process of renewal inside the Communist Party. In retrospect, this had already begun in late 1985 when Nguyen Van Linh, summarily dismissed from the Politburo at the fifth party congress in 1982, was reinstated to the party's highest decision-making body.[17] In the highly conservative world of the inner sanctums of Vietnamese communism, it was inevitable that the next-ranking Politburo member, Truong Chinh, should step into Le Duan's shoes. What was not to be anticipated was the shake-up in the party leadership that took place at the sixth congress in December 1986.[18]

Not only did Truong Chinh step down from the leadership, but he was joined in retirement by the two other senior Politburo members, Le Duc Tho and Pham Van Dong. Three other Politburo members were dropped – Van Tien Dung, the architect of the 1975 military victory, General Chu Huy Man and To Huu. The new party leader was Nguyen Van Linh. Drastic changes were also announced at the congress in the party's secretariat and Central Committee. Only three of the thirteen-member secretariat appointed at the previous congress in 1982 were retained. At the time, the changes announced at the sixth congress were almost without precedent in the history of any ruling communist party. The recognition of the need for even more thoroughgoing changes was indicated when the party frankly admitted its culpability for 'mistakes and shortcomings' in leadership. The political report flatly blamed the leadership for their failings.

The resignation of the party's three senior leaders at the sixth congress reflected a profound internal crisis that had been maturing within the Vietnamese Communist Party for some years. The crisis stemmed from the inability of its ageing leadership to deal with mounting domestic and external problems. Domestically, the economic policies pursued since unification in 1976 had met with almost total failure and the country was being effectively kept afloat by the Soviet Union. Moreover, the accession to power in the Soviet Union in March 1985 of Mikhail Gorbachev indicated that the cosy relationship Vietnamese leaders had enjoyed with Brezhnev and his immediate successors was coming to an end. Externally, Vietnam's invasion of Cambodia in December 1978 had led it into virtual international isolation. Since the last party congress in 1982, these two problems had grown considerably worse. Half-hearted attempts at reform in the early 1980s had, if anything, compounded the country's economic problems, with Vietnam registering a staggering 700% annual inflation and a record budget deficit in 1986. Nor was there any sign of Vietnam being able to extricate itself from the Cambodian quagmire.

The conjunction of Vietnam's international isolation and its grinding economic misery – it was classified by the United Nations as one of the world's twenty poorest countries in the mid-1980s – contributed to a growing malaise not only in the country but within the party itself. An increasingly frank debate ensued. In May, Le Duc Tho wrote a remarkable critique of the party's shortcomings in the pages of its theoretical journal, *Tap Chi Cong San* (Communist Review).[19] In a damning indictment of party life, he wrote of sycophancy and opportunism poisoning the party and of corruption 'tainting every level'. One of the most significant aspects of the article was his frank admission of the age problem. As he put it himself, many senior cadres 'are now too old to be able to do much work'. The party leadership adopted a patriarchal attitude towards younger people, forgetting that when it seized power in 1945 few of its leaders were then more than thirty years old. The article was all the more significant given that its author had been at the heart of Vietnamese communist politics for almost four decades.

In the aftermath of the sixth party congress, as outlined in Chapter 4, Vietnam moved falteringly ahead with economic reform. Within two years it was to have moved further along that road than most other communist states existing at that time. But while there was general recognition in the party of the need for what was euphemistically called 'economic renovation' or *doi moi*, reformists did not have things all their own way. While Linh himself had impeccable reformist credentials, the congress had elected to number two position on the Politburo a highly conservative figure, Pham Hung, who had earned a reputation as a hardliner since he had become Interior Minister in 1980. Moreover, there was an extraordinary delay in replacing Pham Van Dong and Truong Chinh as Prime Minister and President respectively. Thus, for six months after the sixth party congress, Vietnam was in the highly anomalous position for a communist country that its head of government and head of state no longer held senior party positions. This was finally rectified in June 1987, when Pham Hung was appointed Prime Minister, while his old position as Interior Minister was taken by another conservative, Mai Chi Tho, younger brother of Le Duc Tho. Although Pham Hung was to die in office within nine months of his appointment, his election as Prime Minister underlined the continuing delicate balance within the leadership between reformers and conservatives. In 1987, and again in March 1988 following Pham Hung's death, speculation had been rife that Linh would have preferred as Prime Minister his fellow architect of economic reforms in the South, Vo Van Kiet. This reward, however, did not come Kiet's way until August 1991.

The reform programme adopted by the Vietnamese Communist Party in December 1986 was accompanied the following year by a clean-up campaign within the party itself. The campaign, launched in September 1987, was designed to rid party and government ranks of all those deemed to be 'corrupt and degraded'. At the time the party newspaper, *Nhan Dan* (People's Daily), acknowledged that never before had 'morale been so eroded, confidence been so low or justice been so abused'. Even by the standards of glasnost, or greater openness, adopted since 1986, the editorial was striking in its indictment of party and government shortcomings.

The launching of the reform programme, known in Vietnamese as *doi moi*, at the sixth party congress in December 1986 led to a greater tolerance and pluralism in the arts, the media and religion. Glasnost had come to Vietnam. One of the first signs of this was the appearance of articles in *Nhan Dan* under the byline 'NVL', the initials of course of party leader, Nguyen Van Linh. The articles pressed the need for economic reform, urged greater democracy in party life and strongly criticized middle-level bureaucrats who were resisting the tide of reform. It remains unclear whether the articles were written from a position of political strength or weakness. In many ways they had a Gorbachevian ring to them of appealing to the people against the conservative hierarchy. Linh himself acknowledged authorship of the articles in October

1987, telling one interviewer that the initials stood for *noi va lam* ('speak and act'). The important point, however, was that the appearance of the 'NVL' articles gave journalists and the media generally an apparently high-level endorsement to be more critical of the established order.[20]

The 'NVL' articles underlined the commitment of Linh to the reform programme and led to the adoption of a more open press policy. The first article appeared on 25 May 1987. For several months the articles urging the public to act against bureaucratic tyrants and bullies produced only a dreadful silence. But by August 1987 the party daily was receiving 600 letters a month denouncing various government agencies and officials. The fight initiated by 'NVL' against corruption and abuse of power encouraged private and public criticism of public policy that fuelled a more liberal governing trend. The press was particularly affected and became a more aggressive critic of government policy.[21] In some cases it was instrumental in removing local party bosses who had flagrantly abused power and obstructed reforms. In the first six months of 1988, no fewer than 1,100 party cadres were tried for corruption, often after they had been exposed in the press.[22]

The openness with which Vietnam's leaders addressed their own and others' shortcomings in the press in 1987–8 was unparalleled. A party directive from the Central Committee in September 1987 emphasized that not only journalists, but every party member and citizen, had the right to criticize officials guilty of wrongdoing. It also warned officials against attempting to harass or punish those who documented their shortcomings in the press.[23]

In August 1987 an editorial in *Nhan Dan* described the struggle for economic reform and renovation as a matter of life and death for Vietnamese society. In December the same year a communiqué following a ten-day meeting of the Communist Party Central Committee painted a gloomy picture of economic hardship and political mismanagement. The press talked of a serious slump in grain production, and constant shortages; of falling industrial growth and declining standards of living. In an astounding condemnation of its own failures, the party communiqué, which received wider attention in the media than usual, held the leadership responsible for the crisis in Vietnam, accusing itself of bureaucratic, incompetent and indisciplined centralism. And in a quite remarkable call for any ruling communist party to make, it appealed for a struggle against the state of the bureaucracy and its oppression of the masses.[24]

The initial openness in the press came from *Nhan Dan*. But the trend to a more critical press soon spread to Ho Chi Minh City, with *Saigon*

Giai Phong (Saigon Liberation) running a column written by its own readers entitled 'Speaking Frankly and Truthfully'. Another Saigon newspaper, *Tuoi Tre* (Youth), opened a complaints department with reporters assigned to investigate readers' problems.[25] Issues such as drug addiction, prostitution and draft evasion, which were simply not discussed in the press before 1987, now became the subject of heated debate. Western culture, previously covered only in a critical fashion, was now written about in a more dispassionate manner. Even beauty contests became the subject of a column in *Nhan Dan*.

The greater freedom accorded the press from 1987 was extended also to the arts. Western music and videos previously vigorously suppressed were now openly tolerated. For years western pop music and culture had been decried by the authorities. Even ballroom dancing was banned, much to the resentment of many Vietnamese and particularly those in the south of the country. The ageing northern leadership seemed to be imbued not just with the Leninist concept of creating a 'new socialist man' but also with the Confucian ethic of self-restraint. All this now changed, with western culture being tolerated in both its popular and elitist forms. One of the most important factors in contributing to the more relaxed attitude on the part of the authorities was the growing realization that most young Vietnamese were deeply disillusioned by the austere regime hitherto imposed by the Communist Party. It increasingly seemed to be counter-productive to repress western culture. Soon rock music was heard as frequently on the streets of Vietnamese cities as in other parts of Southeast Asia. 'Video-cafés' became part of the scene in Hanoi and Ho Chi Minh City. Books by western writers became more generally available, and Vietnamese writers and film-makers gathered confidence and soon began to challenge the country's social and economic problems.[26]

As economic reform gathered pace after the 1986 congress, so, too, although in a more restricted fashion, did the debate on how Vietnam should be ruled. Increasing attention was given to the need to frame a legal code, with much of the impetus coming from the work of economic renovation. In part, Vietnam may have been influenced by the legal reforms being implemented by President Gorbachev in the Soviet Union. His priority was to establish a framework that would make impossible any return to the arbitrary terror of Stalinism, the cynical manipulation by the state of legal rights and obligations. Gorbachev recognized that, without codification into law, reforms were meaningless, new freedoms and human rights ever hostage to the capricious interpretation of bureaucrats and party functionaries.

To a degree even greater than in other communist countries, Vietnam has been directly governed for decades by the Communist Party, with minimum legal safeguards for citizens. Local cadres exercised extraordinary powers in the areas in which they ruled, and resentment against this state of affairs rapidly came to the surface in the more relaxed atmosphere after 1986. Moreover, the architects of economic reform recognized the need for legal reforms not only to protect the citizen, but also to force recalcitrant cadres to implement the reforms themselves. The focus of the debate on legal reform after 1986 centred on the National Assembly, which increasingly paid more attention to the drafting and promulgation of laws.[27]

Little more than a rubber-stamp body before 1986, the National Assembly had passed few laws from its creation in 1946 until 1980. Between 1980 and 1987, however, it succeeded in adopting twenty laws and decrees. In 1988 it managed to pass eighteen laws, including a Criminal Procedure Code affirming the principle of presumed innocence and setting out the procedures governing the arrest and detention of suspects. This pace was maintained in 1989–90. Many of the laws enacted were closely tied to the economic reforms, which had underlined the need to put in place basic laws on tax, labour and the exploitation of natural resources if Vietnam's economic renovation and its efforts to attract foreign investors were to succeed. But perhaps the key pieces of legislation for Vietnam's citizens over the past decade were the Penal Code and the Code of Penal Procedure. The National Assembly has also set itself the goal of overhauling the country's constitution, with the stated aim of bringing about a formal separation of powers between the Communist Party, the government and the National Assembly itself.[28]

Vietnam's progress in enacting legal reforms was acknowledged by the human rights organization Amnesty International in a report in February 1990.[29] The report welcomed moves towards the creation of an independent judiciary, the introduction of the judicial principle that a defendant is presumed innocent until proven guilty by the court, and a defendant's right to legal defence by an independent lawyer. In May 1989 an Amnesty delegation visited Vietnam for the first time in ten years to discuss legal reform and human rights violations, an indication in itself of the more international attitude prevailing in the country.

One of the results of *doi moi* was that the authorities paid greater attention to international criticism of Vietnam's human rights record. Nguyen Van Linh is reported to have argued forcefully at a Politburo meeting in August 1987 against Interior Minister Mai Chi Tho for the release of all political prisoners.[30] Nearly 500 high-level prisoners from the former South Vietnamese government were released in September 1987 and another 3,820 were granted amnesty for the Tet (New Year) celebrations in February 1988. Moreover, the new Criminal Procedure Code contains no provision for detention without trial and it appears to render untried detention for 're-education' illegal. Amnesty International has also acknowledged steps taken by the government to prevent torture and ill-treatment and the denunciation of such abuses by the media.

A stronger legal framework meant greater protection not only for individuals, but also for ethnic and religious minorities. This was particularly the case for Vietnam's Chinese minority, whose members had undergone considerable discrimination and repression in 1978–9 as Hanoi's relations with Peking deteriorated. In a meeting in July 1987 with several prominent Chinese citizens in Ho Chi Minh City, Linh stressed that the Chinese community was 'protected by court of law'.[31] New decrees affecting ethnic Chinese assure them of the same rights as Vietnamese citizens. As with other legal reforms, the new measures had an economic dimension. Hanoi now needed the skills of the ethnic Chinese if its economic reforms were to be a success.

Setback to reform: the 1989 crisis

In the course of 1989 the considerable gains that *doi moi* had brought Vietnam since the sixth party congress came under threat. The crisis of international communism in China, the Soviet Union and Eastern Europe inevitably had an enormous impact on the party leadership in Hanoi, which had long prided itself on its 'internationalism'. Domestic factors, too, contributed to a rigorous application of the brakes to the whole reform process. The results were severe, especially in the realm of social and political reform.

Signs of a conservative backlash were already evident in 1988. In June that year the reformer Vo Van Kiet failed in a bid to win the premiership, losing in a ballot in the National Assembly to the more conservative Do Muoi.[32] A number of writers had also been arrested.[33] The hardening mood was obvious in February 1989 when Nguyen Van Linh addressed newspaper editors and journalists in Ho Chi Minh City. He warned the country's media against publishing reports that caused a loss of confidence in the Communist Party or the government. At the same time he delivered the first of several warnings that there could be no question of political pluralism developing in Vietnam. The press, Linh

31

argued, had to remain a tool of the Communist Party even while reflecting the views of the people. Significantly, articles by Comrade 'NVL' had stopped appearing in *Nhan Dan* several months earlier. Two months before Linh's warning to the press, an article had appeared in the party theoretical journal, *Tap Chi Cong San*, by Interior Minister Mai Chi Tho, accusing the press of ideological laxity and commercialization. Behind this intervention many saw the hand of Mai Chi Tho's elder brother, Le Duc Tho, who, although no longer on the Politburo, still exercised enormous informal influence over the party. The limits of reform in Vietnam had, for the time being, been reached. Henceforth, while there was faltering endorsement of economic renovation, glasnost was under wraps.[34]

The concern of the leadership that economic reform and the more relaxed atmosphere which had been obvious since 1986 might get out of hand increased as a result of a series of student demonstrations in May and June 1989. Although largely concerned with demands for better housing and educational facilities, the students were almost certainly influenced by the wave of student unrest in China at the time. More striking and strident were the comments that began appearing from July on developments in Poland and Hungary. Criticism of the moves in those countries towards greater democracy and political pluralism was among the strongest made by any ruling communist party at the time. The Vietnamese media presented them as an attack by imperialist forces to subvert socialism. It was notable that the media in covering the events of June 1989 in Peking had given attention only to the Chinese authorities' account, despite Vietnam's long alienation from China.

In August the Communist Party's Central Committee met in Ho Chi Minh City for their seventh plenum to tackle what were called 'urgent ideological problems'. In a communiqué published at the end of the meeting, the party strongly attacked bourgeois liberalism and accused the United States of attempting to undermine socialism worldwide. It went on to rule out any prospect of political reform and denounced such measures in other socialist societies as being little more than attempts to restore capitalism. In a closing speech at the conference, Nguyen Van Linh went out of his way to threaten severe punishment for those who organized or incited civil unrest. He also admitted that there had been widespread ideological confusion within the ranks of the party as a result of the events in Eastern Europe. Indeed the call in the official communiqué to strengthen the forces of international socialism only underlined the growing isolation of the Vietnamese Communist Party from the profound changes under way within most of the communist world itself. Having closely aligned themselves with the Soviet Union and Eastern Europe for years, Vietnam's leaders seemed at pains to distance themselves from their hitherto closest allies.[35]

The seventh plenum was followed by a further tightening of restrictions on the press. Some journals were closed and the editors of others were replaced. Before the opening of the journalists' association congress on 15 October, *Nhan Dan* warned of what it called the press's shortcomings. At the congress itself, Prime Minister Do Muoi spoke of the duty of journalists to 'struggle against reactionary forces and thoughts that sabotage the revolutionary gains of the country'. In December a motion at the National Assembly to allow private individuals to publish newspapers was heavily defeated and a controversial new press law was introduced making it an offence 'to make propaganda' against the Communist Party and socialism.[36] The publications of the Club of Former Resistance Fighters, a dissident group based in Ho Chi Minh City, were also banned.

At the same time attempts by hardline conservatives to consolidate their hold on the party leadership still met with resistance. Attacks on the concept of political pluralism increased in the party press. But, despite the shockwaves felt in Hanoi at the rapid and dramatic collapse of communism in Eastern Europe, some elements clearly felt that battening down the hatches was not the answer. The deputy editor of *Nhan Dan*, Colonel Bui Tin, warned openly that if antagonisms between the people and the party were not resolved, a political crisis similar to those that had beset the Czechoslovak and Romanian communist parties might be unavoidable. More striking still was a speech in December 1989 by the Politburo member responsible for relations with other communist parties, Tran Xuan Bach. He called for greater openness and added that it was absurd to think that Asian communism was immune to the changes taking place in Eastern Europe. While giving no indication that he opposed one-party rule, he stressed that political reform had to accompany economic liberalization.

His advocacy of greater political reform lost Bach his positions on both the Politburo and the Central Committee at the eighth party plenum in March 1990. This unprecedented action, removing a key Politburo member in between party congresses, was undoubtedly motivated by growing fears among the leadership that Vietnam would indeed not be immune to the contagion of political reform that had swept Eastern Europe and the Soviet Union.[37] The Vietnamese party had been closely allied to the Soviet and East European parties since 1975. More specifically, it had tied its political fortunes from the late 1970s firmly to the Soviet Union, even to the extent of becoming a member of Comecon. Now the structures of the international communist world were collapsing and the very status of the Soviet Union as a superpower was being brought into question. Moreover, to conservatives in the leadership in Hanoi, the dangers of economic reform eroding the basis of the Communist Party's monopoly of political power began to appear very real.

That possibility already seemed distinct with the appearance on the edges of the Communist Party for the first time of dissident political activity. In May 1986 the Club of Former Resistance Fighters had been formed in Ho Chi Minh City, bringing together many former prominent figures in the National Liberation Front. By 1988 the Club had begun making trenchant criticisms of the Communist Party, calling for greater openness, intra-party democracy and the serious implementation of *doi moi*. Attempts by the southern veterans to link up with counterparts in the North seem to have been the last straw for the leadership in Hanoi, which reacted, as noted, by banning the Club's publications and forming a tame veterans' organization firmly under party control.[38]

More serious still for the party was the defection to the West in late 1990 of Colonel Bui Tin, the former deputy editor of *Nhan Dan* and the officer who had taken the surrender of South Vietnamese forces at the former presidential palace in Saigon in 1975. In a series of extended interviews with the BBC Vietnamese Service, Bui Tin strongly criticized the Communist Party for not moving fast enough with economic reforms and for retaining its dictatorial use of political power. He was later expelled from the party, as was the writer Duong Thu Huong, who in addition was imprisoned for several months. Less radical criticisms of party policy and performance were also made in the run-up to the seventh party congress in 1991 by prominent intellectuals, such as the historian Nguyen Khac Vien and the mathematician Phan Dinh Dieu.[39]

The seventh party congress
By the beginning of 1991, the conservative counter-reaction that had been so strong since the seventh plenum in August 1989 was waning. It was clear even to diehards that there could be no reversal of economic reform and that to do so might provoke the challenge to Communist Party rule that they so feared. It had also become increasingly clear that the winds of change that had swept Eastern Europe in 1989 were bringing

into question Communist Party rule in the Soviet Union itself. Finally, the death of Le Duc Tho in 1990 had robbed conservatives of a possible rallying figure. Visits to Moscow by Nguyen Van Linh and Prime Minister Do Muoi in May 1991 seem to have convinced the leadership in Hanoi that it could no longer count on political, let alone economic, support from the Soviet Union and that the rigorous pursuit of economic reform was the best course for survival for the Vietnamese Communist Party.[40] It was against this background that the party held its much delayed seventh congress in Hanoi in late June.

The congress resulted in major changes in the leadership and saw a reaffirmation of the commitment to economic reform. Linh resigned as party leader and was replaced by Prime Minister Do Muoi.[41] Six other Politburo members also resigned, including the reformist Foreign Minister Nguyen Co Thach and the hardline Interior Minister Mai Chi Tho. Only five members of the old Politburo were retained on the new thirteen-member body. In general, the balance of forces on the new Politburo seemed to tilt in favour of reformists, and by Vietnamese standards they are much younger, the majority being in their mid-sixties. Several factors need to be borne in mind, however.

Similar changes occurred at the last party congress, the sixth, in December 1986. That congress elected Linh as leader and launched Vietnam on a course of economic reform. The new party leader, Do Muoi, is, at 74 years old, only two years younger than Linh. His previous reputation was as a conservative and he is remembered in southern Vietnam as one of the architects of the 'socialist transformation' after the end of the war in 1975. His experience of the outside world is, apart from a few trips to India, confined to the communist bloc. Since his appointment in 1988 as Prime Minister, however, he has shown a pragmatic attitude towards economic reform. Nevertheless, the appointment disappointed most Vietnamese, who do not see him as the sort of leader who will take the country into the twenty-first century. In many ways, he is less committed to reform than Linh. The number two in the party leadership is General Le Duc Anh, who played a key role in the Vietnamese military intervention in Cambodia. It is the first time that a military man has risen to such a high rank in the party. He is widely regarded as conservative and has voiced fears about the growth of dissent. It is likely that he will oppose major cuts in the defence budget and in the size of the army, still one of the largest in the world.

The congress reaffirmed its commitment to economic reform, but, shaken by the collapse of communism in Eastern Europe, firmly rejected any idea of political pluralism. On the contrary, its espousal of the Communist Party's monopoly of political power was as loud as its recognition of the need for economic reform. The key reformers in the present leadership are Vo Van Kiet, Phan Van Khai, formerly head of the State Planning Commission, and Vo Tran Chi, the former party boss in Ho Chi Minh City. All have extensive experience in the South, where the economic reforms have had greater impact. The leaders are younger now, but the improvement is only relative. The average age of Politburo members has come down from 71 to 64, and that of Central Committee members is 57, with only three members 45 or younger in a country where more than 50% of the population is under the age of 21.[42]

The problems and contradictions that now confront the Communist Party were evident in Do Muoi's closing speech and in the political report earlier of his predecessor, Nguyen Van Linh. Thus, on the one hand Do Muoi said that economic reform was the keynote of party policy, while on the other he stressed the party's unshakable determination to follow the path of socialism. These contradictions were even more evident in Linh's political report, which was an eloquent testimony to the painful choices facing the party. It mixed recognition of the need for glasnost with calls for discipline and enhanced centralism, greater democracy with a thorough rejection of any sort of pluralism, endorsement of a multi-sector economy with the demand that all key industries remain under state control. The party's prestige and popularity in Vietnam is undoubtedly at its lowest ebb. Linh himself spoke of the 'overall profound crisis of socialism', reflecting the continued shock in Vietnam at the collapse of communism in Eastern Europe and the decline of the Soviet Union. But, unless the party is able to push ahead rapidly with economic reform and show a tangible rise in living standards within a few years, the risk of social unrest, especially in the South, is great.

In the wake of the party congress, a major reshuffle in the government took place in August 1991. Extensive though the reshuffle was, there were few real surprises in the new cabinet line-up announced at a session of the National Assembly. Most of the changes had been widely rumoured since the party congress in late June. Undoubtedly the appointment of the highly respected Vo Van Kiet as Prime Minister will give a desperately needed boost for reform and a move towards a more open market economy. In an address to the National Assembly, Mr Kiet was unequivocal in stressing that the state itself had no option but to encourage private enterprise and market reforms. A southerner by background and an architect of early economic reforms there in the 1980s, Kiet is widely seen as one of the few members of the ruling Politburo with a thorough grasp of the dire economic realities facing Vietnam. In confronting these realities, he will be ably assisted by the new first deputy Prime Minister Phan Van Khai, who was the only other serious candidate for the premiership. Like Kiet, Phan Van Khai is firmly convinced of the urgent need for economic reform.

Committed though these two men are to the cause of economic reform, they have to act within a leadership which is collegiate and which maintains a delicate balance between reformers and conservatives. There are probably no more than five clear reformers on the ruling thirteen-man Politburo; the preoccupation with balance in the leadership can be seen from some of the other ministerial changes announced in August.

The influence of the military, in Vietnam as in China a conservative force, has increased both in the government and in the party leadership. The new Defence Minister is General Doan Khue. He takes over from General Le Duc Anh, who, as noted, emerged at the party congress in June as number two in the Politburo. It is widely expected that General Anh will eventually take over as head of state from Vo Chi Cong. The new Interior Minister is also a military man, Lieutenant General Bui Thien Ngo. Although his predecessor, Mai Chi Tho, was a conservative, he was not from the military. This heavy concentration of military men is likely to find reflection in opposition not only to cuts in the size of the armed forces but to any move towards greater pluralism or multi-party democracy.

Not, however, that political reform can be entirely removed from the agenda – as the seventh congress made clear. Indeed, there seems to be a consensus among the leadership that a measure of political reform is now vital, both for the success of economic reform and in order to stave off any potential challenge to the party's monopoly of political power. There was also a notable attempt at the seventh congress to emphasize the distinctiveness and national character of Vietnamese communism. Thus while the congress ritually reaffirmed its adherence to Marxism-Leninism, despite the recent rejection of Marx and Lenin in Germany and Russia, it at the same time stressed the importance of 'the thoughts of Ho Chi Minh'.[43] In this connection, it is interesting to note the celebrations that attended the centenary of Ho Chi Minh's birth in 1990 and the opening of impressive new museums devoted to his life in Hanoi and Ho Chi Minh City.

As noted, by the time of the seventh congress, concern for its own survival increasingly seemed to push the leadership in the direction of a measure of political reform. This entailed greater inner party democracy by, for example, introducing secret ballots and providing for a party conference to be held before the next party congress. Rumours suggest that this conference, a favourite tactical weapon of Mikhail Gorbachev to rout party conservatives in the past, could take place as early as 1993 and that the current party leader, Do Muoi, might take that moment to step down from office in favour of a younger man.

As for wider democratic measures, the party appears to be reconciled to seeing its role in the state reduced. The number of party supervisory committees, which oversee ministries, has been greatly reduced, and constitutional amendments, which have been under discussion throughout 1991, envisage a more powerful prime minister and executive cabinet. Vo Van Kiet has said that he does not rule out the possibility of appointing non-communists to positions in the cabinet.[44] These amendments would also see the National Assembly enjoying a more prominent role. However, the postponement of decisions about these amendments at a plenum of the party Central Committee in December 1991 indicates that conservatives are still unhappy with the proposed democratic changes. The amendments to the constitution, which have been through at least three drafts, were discussed by the Central Committee and ratified by the National Assembly on 15 April 1992.[45] Elections for a new national assembly, under the provisions of the new laws, are expected to take place in mid-1992, but the delays in enacting the legislative amendments underline once again the fears of many in the party leadership that political reform will inevitably dilute the Communist Party's monopoly of power.

4

REFORM AND THE ECONOMY

The fate of the Vietnamese Communist Party is inextricably linked to the fortunes of *doi moi*, economic renovation. Of the world's remaining communist states – Vietnam, China, North Korea and Cuba – Vietnam's leadership, even compared with that of China, has made the strongest commitment to economic reform. Agriculture and the retail trade have effectively been privatized, the country has one of the most liberal foreign investment codes in East Asia and price controls have for the most part been abolished. The regime of neo-Stalinist central planning erected in the 1960s and 1970s has to all intents and purposes been dismantled, and the country is well on the way to becoming a market economy.[1] This process has gone much further than had even the successful reforming communist economies in Eastern Europe, such as Hungary and Poland, prior to autumn 1989. Indeed one of the most knowledgeable observers of the Vietnamese economy, Adam Fforde, claims that Vietnam provides 'the sole example in the world today of a ruling Communist Party that has managed to abandon the central-planning methods derived from Stalinist Russia'.[2] These reforms have won plaudits from the International Monetary Fund.

While the move towards a market economy started with the sixth party congress in 1986, it accelerated in 1989, when the remnants of the centrally planned economy were discarded in favour of an outward-looking market-oriented development model. The recent seventh congress again reasserted the leadership's commitment to economic reform and, in the 'Strategy for Socioeconomic Stabilization and Development' adopted at the congress, pledged itself to privatization and using 'all possibilities and different methods of attracting foreign capital'.[3] The collapse of the trading bloc Comecon, and of the Soviet Union itself, have further weakened the central planning mechanism by effectively making redundant existing state to state contracts.

The move away from a centrally planned economy has led to a modest improvement in the quality of life of most Vietnamese: rationing has virtually disappeared, comparatively cheap consumer goods are abundant and, for those with money, access to foreign exchange is relatively easy. At the same time, for those in employment, real incomes appear to have risen significantly over the past ten years. In essence, Vietnam is already a market economy. Most capital is now controlled by economic units that primarily seek to use it for commercial ends, that is to buy and sell in markets profitably.[4] Although the economy still faces many substantial problems, not least the continuing American embargo which denies it complete integration into the international economy, its success so far against severe odds gives room for guarded optimism. Quite apart from the formal economy, there exists an enormous informal economy which has always been present but which has grown considerably as a result of the more liberal atmosphere prevailing since 1986. Fed by smuggling and overseas remittances, it accounts for anything up to 50% of the country's real GNP. It is this which gives Vietnam's economy its extraordinary resilience and ability to survive seemingly insurmountable odds. What does seem clear is that a retreat to the old Stalinist orthodoxies already looks out of the question economically without raising the spectre of widespread social and probably political opposition. If the leadership in Hanoi can feel some satisfaction at the economic progress of recent years, it is important to remember that its past performance has been one of a catalogue of lost opportunities and false starts from 1975 onwards.

Socialist transformation of the economy after 1975

With the end of the war in 1975, Vietnam achieved the national unity and independence for which hundreds of thousands of lives had been shed in the preceding three decades. Its leaders were presented with the opportunity for the first time in over a century of harmonizing the two halves of the country free from foreign interference. Even given the Marxist-Leninist orthodoxies which then prevailed in Hanoi, the option existed for maintaining a mixed economy in the South, for which ideological justification could have been found in Lenin's New Economic Policy (NEP). Such a move would have found much support in the South and would have helped staunch the haemorrhage of boat-people that were soon to leave the country. A maintenance of the economic status quo in the South would also have enabled the country as a whole to have more immediate access to international development assistance. The course of events, however, was to be otherwise.

Revolutionary euphoria, ideological inflexibility and a scarcely veiled contempt for the 'soft' ways of the South dictated an uncompromising line from the leadership in Hanoi. The party clearly believed that recent enemies should be driven out of the economy as soon as possible. Nor were the lessons of economic difficulties brought about by the rapid transformation of the North in the immediate period following the long struggle against the French taken into account. The Stalinist-derived economic system that had operated in the North for some twenty years was rigidly applied over the two halves of the country, which had not even had trading relations for three decades. Not surprisingly, in what should have been a period of reconstruction for the Vietnamese economy, the country suffered an economic decline. A sense of economic failure and disillusionment with the Communist Party's handling of the unification process eventually served as a stimulus for a reform of the economic system. However, this was to prove a long and drawn-out process, during which time the economy teetered on the brink of collapse.

The decision to incorporate the economy of the South into the state plan should not be seen in purely economic terms. The main motive for its implementation was political. The choice as to whether the South should immediately begin the socialist phase of its development or be allowed first to complete the pre-socialist phase was made by a party leadership in Hanoi whose chief concern was to discourage any notion that the South might follow a non-socialist path of development.[5] It had been envisaged that a provisional revolutionary government would endeavour to bring about a national reconciliation and a reconstruction of the economy in the South in the postwar period. The southern economy was primarily agricultural and operated according to the rules of the market. Establishing a new administrative mechanism that facilitated central control of what was basically a free enterprise system was to prove difficult in the aftermath of war, especially given the critical shortage of experienced cadres in the South.

By embarking on an early unification of the two halves of the country and thereby forcing the South to adopt the North's economic practices, the Hanoi leadership effectively reduced the capability of the economy to expand output at the very time when this was most needed. It also closed the door to many of the external economic relationships that the South enjoyed with the wider non-communist economic community. Nevertheless, the confidence of the party in the revolutionary atmosphere of 1975 was such as to expect not only a quick recovery from war, but also a rapid march towards socialism.

This was to be elaborated formally in the Second Five-Year Plan (1976–80), adopted at the fourth party congress in 1976. Orthodox Soviet institutions were established throughout the country in a manner not dissimilar to that used in Eastern Europe in the late 1940s, or China in the 1950s. The thrust of the plan, designed to integrate the two halves of the country, was to leave the richer South concentrating on agriculture and the North on industry. The hope was that the countryside would subsidize the economic development of industries in the towns. The plan, however, took little account of the resistance of the peasantry in the South to collectivization and was anyway far too ambitious in thinking that the land would generate sufficient surpluses to fund industrialization. It also took insufficient account of the damage inflicted on the country by decades of war. Finally, in its hopes for international funding of postwar economic reconstruction, it was wildly optimistic.

A failure to establish diplomatic relations with the United States after the war can in part be attributed to Hanoi's mishandling of the issue of a US undertaking in 1973 to provide economic assistance in the immediate postwar era. By the time Hanoi realized that it had miscalculated, the mood in Washington had changed and the Carter administration had other foreign policy priorities. Only modest amounts of foreign investment were forthcoming from other western countries, notably Sweden. It was anticipated that the Soviet Union and China would be willing to supply nearly two-thirds of a total investment figure of over $7 billion, with the remainder being provided by the West. But the economic planners had not foreseen a weakening relationship with both China and the wider international community. As it turned out, even before the Second Five-Year Plan could be completed, Vietnam became increasingly embroiled in hostilities with the Khmer Rouge regime in Cambodia, which would lead to additional economic burdens for the country and the ending of Chinese economic aid.

The cost of Vietnam's December 1978 invasion of Cambodia is difficult to assess. However, it is clear that the burden of support for the newly installed regime in Phnom Penh proved a considerable drain on the country's economy. The intervention in Cambodia inevitably brought a hostile reaction from China, which brought an end to cross-border trade as well as to aid from Peking. But most damaging of all was Vietnam's complete isolation from the world economy as a result of the war in Cambodia. The American-led embargo was now joined by all western countries, except Sweden, and by ASEAN.

In desperate need of economic assistance on an ever larger scale, Vietnam developed a much closer relationship with the Soviet bloc. In 1978 Vietnam was accepted as the tenth member of Comecon. If it had not been for the aid and assistance provided by the Soviet Union in the next seven years, the economy would probably have suffered a collapse long before the reform process began to register improvements in the domestic situation. The move into Cambodia ensured that the trend which had seen an increasing slice of government revenue being devoted to the military budget was reinforced. Over a third of government expenditure during the 1976–80 plan is believed to have been allocated to the military budget. This was a major drain on an economic system that already relied on Hanoi receiving some 40% of its revenue from external aid and assistance. What growth there was in the economy was more than eaten up by population increase, resulting in a drop in per capita income. At the same time, military ranks had swelled to a figure of around one million.

By the end of the decade the leadership was forced to reassess economic policy in order to try and register some improvement in the economic situation of a population that was becoming rapidly disillusioned with the party's handling of affairs. The negative effects of forced socialization in the South, the campaign against capitalist trade and the treatment of the ethnic Chinese caused a dramatic economic downturn. In view of the stagnation of the northern economy, drastic measures to stimulate production were clearly called for. The implementation of such measures proved to be only the initial steps on a road to reform that is transforming the Vietnamese economy from a centrally planned to a market-oriented system.

The road to reform

Like every other road Vietnam seems to have traversed in its modern history, that to reform has been long and tortuous. At the end of the 1970s the Vietnamese economy faced a very real crisis. Quite apart from the punitive international isolation into which the country had been plunged, the rapid industrialization and unrealistic targets set in 1976 had failed to materialize. Behind this failure, there was increasing evidence that, notwithstanding the monolithic façade of party rule, there was far from uniform control, especially in the countryside. Indeed some observers have argued that, even before 1975, party control of the economy in the North was far from what was claimed by official propaganda. Although the Soviet-style institutions necessary to create forced economic development were in place, the compulsion associated with those institutions in classic Stalinist policies seems to have been lacking.[6] The only options, therefore, were either a considerable strengthening of the forces of compulsion or giving way to realities.

Adoption of what was later called the 'bureaucratic centralist system' of economic management led to serious distortions in the functioning of the Vietnamese economy. Production was organized on the basis of detailed plans produced at the centre by the State Planning Commission. There was little in the way of financial discipline, with the requirements of enterprises being met out of the state budget. As the disparity between official prices for goods and those circulating on the free market continued to widen, the system came increasingly to rely on massive subsidies to the state sector in order to prevent it from collapsing. Prices set for raw materials allocated to state enterprises bore little relation to their real value within the economy. Enterprises and other state agencies sought to exploit the distortions in the pricing system by engaging in the illegal resale of goods and materials bought at artificially fixed prices. The agricultural sector was expected to fund the increasing slice of the state budget being devoted to industrial development out of farming surpluses. However, by 1979 it had become clear that the theory was falling down in practice. Not only had the industrial sector ceased to grow, but food production was very unsteady, rising one year, falling the next. Gross National Product was barely equal to that of 1976, while population increase had lowered the per capita figure. Food output rose by only one million tonnes between 1976 and 1980, but dropped per head of population from 274 to 268 kilograms during this time.[7]

By the time the leadership gathered for the sixth plenum of the Fourth Central Committee in August 1979, there was a realization that something had to be done to halt the decline in production levels, particularly with regard to agriculture. The decision to retreat from rapid socialist transformation of the economy and implement a policy of reform paved the way for economic recovery during the 1981–5 Five-Year Plan. Moves to provide material incentives to producers while encouraging individual initiative were introduced in conjunction with the decision to grant greater autonomy to local authorities and production units.[8] Under a new contract system in agriculture, households were allocated land by the collectives. Any output produced above the contracted amount with the collective could be retained or freely sold on the open market. The system brought an average annual increase of nearly one million tonnes of food between 1980 and 1983, about five times the growth rate during the previous five-year plan. By linking the producer to the final product, thereby rewarding farmers for their level of production as opposed to the amount of working time, productivity soared. As that early proponent of reform Vo Van Kiet put it in a speech to the party in 1983, 'an initial change has been wrought in our economy, chiefly in food production ... for the first time we have not had to import food'.[9]

The limited reforms enacted in August 1979 can be seen in retrospect as the beginnings of a move away from the classic Stalinist orthodoxies of the plan. They showed a tactical sensitivity on the part of the leadership to economic realities on the ground. Much of the economy was out of the control of the central authorities in the early 1980s, with agricultural cooperatives starting to break down and an increase in 'unplanned' economic activities within the country and between Vietnam and the outside world. In some quarters of the party, there were growing doubts about the entire central planning system. Nevertheless, conservative elements in the party were able to mount a strong counter-offensive in 1982. The *de facto* independence of many enterprises, not to mention the peasants on the cooperatives, was reined in.

The implied failure of the leadership's policy of rapid socialist transformation in the South gave rise to something of a backlash at the fifth congress in March 1982 against those who had cautioned against it. The most notable casualty was Nguyen Van Linh. As a former party secretary in Ho Chi Minh City, Linh was well placed to appreciate the damage that Hanoi's policies had inflicted on the economy of the Mekong delta. However, politics remained very much in the ascendancy, and as the relationship with China was continuing to prove one of intense hostility, the ethnic Chinese community, the backbone of Ho Chi Minh City's economic prosperity, was a focus of attention for the central authorities. Although he had been unceremoniously dropped from the Politburo, Linh, along with Vo Van Kiet, continued to argue that the socialist transformation of capitalist trade had been a serious mistake, and that the main reason why the state could not meet the needs of the masses for consumer goods was that it was violating economic laws in its pricing policies and its administrative controls over production and distribution.[10] His reinstatement as a Politburo member at a meeting of the central committee in June 1985, and his elevation barely eighteen months later to the post of General Secretary, was vindication of his view that the party's approach to the country's economic problems since unification had been flawed from the beginning.

The meeting set the stage for a package of reform measures that in the following year received the support of the sixth party congress, significantly quickening the pace of *doi moi* in the second half of the 1980s. A resolution adopted at the plenum proposed radical price, wage and currency measures, aimed at renovating the system of economic management. The subsidization of prices and wages would cease as the economy began to operate along business-accounting and socialist enterprise lines. The key to this was seen to be the application of a unified pricing system to serve as a basis for the establishment of a new wage structure. It was envisaged that remuneration would be tied to productivity, product quality and labour efficiency. In addition, financial autonomy was to be accorded to productive, trading and service enterprises, which were to become responsible for their own profits and losses. This would require credit operations to be based on the efficient use of the funds provided. If financial discipline was to be encouraged, indirect mechanisms of control would need to be strengthened. Corruption and waste would therefore have to be identified and tackled accordingly.[11]

In the run-up to the sixth party congress and the adoption of a new Five-Year Plan by the National Assembly, advocates of reform stepped up their campaign for the dismantling of the existing system of economic management in order to encourage initiative in the areas of production and trade. Vo Van Kiet was able to utilize his position as head of the State Planning Commission to try to increase the responsibilities and influence of the districts in the organization and management of the economy. If the renovation process was to succeed, then a distinction had to be drawn between the function of administrative management and that of production and business management. Staffing levels in the bureaucracy would have to be reduced, and many new cadres capable of meeting the challenge of a new economic structure and a new management mechanism would be needed. Not surprisingly, such a process continued to meet stiff opposition from elements within the party and state bureaucracy. This was reflected in a Politburo resolution in September 1985, which fell short of the measures that had been put forward three months earlier.[12] Although in principle endorsing a move towards a one-price system, the two-tier system was not to be abolished at this stage, nor were state subsidies eliminated.

While the party leadership prevaricated over taking the necessary measures required for a restructuring of the economy, the country continued to be plagued by inflation and balance-of-payments deficits. Shortages of goods and materials became more prevalent. In order to stabilize the situation, Hanoi had to deplete further its foreign exchange reserves and allow arrears on debt repayments to continue to mount. Fatefully, the government in 1985 decided not to continue servicing outstanding debts to the IMF. Vietnam's convertible currency debt had been accumulated in the late 1970s to finance food and oil imports and with loans for development purposes.

Increasingly, Vietnam looked to the Soviet Union to bale it out of the economic mire. But Moscow, without whose support the trade deficits could simply not have been funded, appeared less willing to continue propping up the Vietnamese economy once Mikhail Gorbachev came to power in March 1985, although ironically between 1986 and 1990 Soviet economic aid actually increased. Nevertheless, there were growing complaints that corrupt officials continued to siphon off Soviet aid, and that promised reforms designed to put aid and assistance to better use had not been implemented. As Yegor Ligachev pointed out in his capacity as CPSU Politburo delegate to the sixth congress, the aim was to 'ensure that each economic and social objective being erected in Vietnam with the assistance of the USSR should be made operational on time, produce the greatest returns, and facilitate a speedy resolution to the problems facing Vietnam.'[13]

During this whole period Vietnam built up a substantial debt to the Soviet Union. Moscow accounted for about 80% of the value of Vietnam's trade with Comecon and over 60% of the total value of foreign trade. By the end of the Second Five-Year Plan in 1980, Soviet economic aid was equal to the total of the previous four years combined. Aid projects increased significantly throughout the 1980s. The second plan had seen 162 Soviet-funded aid projects. The third plan (1981–5) saw this figure rise to some 300, and the fourth (1986–90) to 550. In addition, military aid to fund the conflict in Cambodia had risen consistently since 1978, peaking at $1.7 billion in 1985.[14] The size of the debt has become the focus of current disagreement between the two former communist allies and is a major problem facing the Vietnamese government in the 1990s. However, isolation from the international community served to limit the scale of the trade deficit with the convertible currency world. The deficit dropped from $481 million in 1981 to $309 million in 1986 as a result of increasing exports of agricultural and marine products to the convertible area, while hard currency imports of food and capital goods were reduced.[15] Against this background, the Communist Party gathered for the sixth congress in December 1986. As the advocates of reform gained the upper hand, the congress was to prove something of a turning-point for the renovation process.

Doi moi comes into its own

The sixth congress reinforced moves towards reform and began the process of generational change within the party leadership. Leadership changes were to some extent a recognition that the earlier reforms had saved the Third Five-Year Plan from repeating the economic failure of the second. With economic problems mounting, the congress gave the go-ahead for a more far-reaching programme of reform and made initial strides in elevating a new generation of technocrats to manage the transition to a market-oriented economy. Since the congress was broadcast live across the country, the party used it as a platform for self-criticism over the failure of policies surrounding the socialist transformation of the economy, and as a launching-pad for *doi moi*.

In his opening address to the congress, Nguyen Van Linh, while pointing to the important achievements and victories recorded in the building of socialism and the defence of the country, stressed the adverse effects:

> We must see even more clearly the reverse side of the situation, especially concerning the socioeconomic field, with sluggishness in production, confusion in distribution and circulation, difficulties in the people's lives, negative phenomena in several aspects of life and a decline in the working people's confidence. These are things that our party as well as our people cannot accept. We must certainly use all means to effect a change in the situation. In particular, we must stabilize the economy and society, make them healthy and take them forward.[16]

The unfolding of the programme of *doi moi* represented a sustained attack on the old model of a centrally planned economy. After 1986 central planning coexisted alongside market-type relations. In that sense the congress represented an important retreat by the party, inasmuch as it was forced to admit that planning had been a failure. The state had failed to implement its own declared policy. Henceforth, the 'bureaucratic subsidy system' was to stand condemned, and the state, and its driving force the Communist Party, took a more positive attitude towards the non-socialist sectors and the free market.

From early 1987 onwards, there was a sharp reduction in internal trade barriers and a liberalization of foreign trade. Both enterprises and local authorities were allowed to carry out direct economic contacts with overseas markets. Subsidies to the state sector to cover operating losses were to be gradually phased out. The state and cooperative sectors were expected to make use of entrepreneurial methods to secure positions for themselves within the market, their performance in the marketplace determining whether they stay in business. On this basis, management was to become responsible for setting its own production and wage levels, and must decide how much of its profit should be allocated to reinvestment. For the first time, enterprises were going to have to balance the books.

Ending subsidies for state enterprises has not proved to be an easy task, and the process has still to be completed. The state sector's inefficiency is seen by many in Vietnam as the main cause of the country's economic difficulties. In 1988, state-owned enterprises still accounted for over 70% of the country's industrial output, 40% of trade, and 85% of fixed assets. Losses still accounted for around 5% of central and local government budgetary expenditures, and the sector was continuing to employ 90% of the country's engineers and specialists.[17] Of course part of the problem is that Vietnam's 'specialists' have not been trained in the ways of the market.[18]

The 1988 crisis

The implementation of the reform process was greatly hampered, however, by inflation, much of it the result of monetary reforms introduced in 1985. Inflationary pressures were exacerbated by substantial government budget deficits and by the chronic inability of the banking system to enforce credit discipline.

With productivity falling and inflation raging, per capita food output dropped in 1987 and resulted the following year in serious food shortages in several northern provinces. Government efforts to purchase rice from the more prosperous areas of the South and transport it to the North ran into difficulties, and some three million people had to survive in near-famine conditions. In addition, the food supplies of a further eight million were dangerously depleted. Now the party leadership was faced with a growing crisis. Inadequate food supplies and rampant inflation were inflicting suffering on the population on a scale not seen since the late 1970s. The consequences of an inefficient centrally planned policy, and especially the growing losses in the state industrial enterprise sector, called into question not only the party's competence but also its legitimacy to rule. The deteriorating situation was reflected in a new wave of boat-people departures.

With industrial output falling, a shortage of goods continued to fuel inflation. By April 1988, a kilogram of high-quality rice cost 600 dong, compared with only 30 dong two years previously.[19] Inflation was running into triple digits again. This rampant inflation had very severe consequences. It undermined real wages and savings, created havoc in the management of the government budget, and had a devastating effect on agriculture, upsetting the contract system and leading to a considerable drop in rice production.

In an effort to boost agricultural production, the government moved in early 1988 to reform the 'output contract' system. By this measure the role of the cooperatives was drastically reduced, increasing the freedom of farmers and effectively moving towards the official acceptance of the family farm as the basic socioeconomic unit in the countryside. The leadership underlined its determination on the issue by instructing provincial and district cadres not to interfere with lawful private activities. In April, at the first national congress of the Vietnamese Peasants' Association, Nguyen Van Linh went out of his way to praise the positive role of private farmers. In the weeks that followed, collectives throughout the country were scaled down in size, or simply replaced by private farming. Around 50% of the cadre jobs in cooperatives and collectives were sacrificed. The weak link of the Vietnamese economy had been addressed. Within a year, Vietnamese agriculture was to show a remarkable turnaround.[20]

At the same time, small-scale private enterprise began to flourish in the towns, especially in Ho Chi Minh City, where, according to one estimate, some 3,000 private shops employing 30,000 workers were established in the first six months of 1987 alone.[21] The informal sector of the economy suddenly opened up. Dollars, gold and goods that had been hoarded for years were finally put to good use. Enterprises that were nominally state-owned began to operate under new business-accounting schemes, thereby acquiring unprecedented independence and the ability to engage in trade and even joint investments with foreign enterprises. The latter was made much easier after the promulgation of a new foreign

investment code in December 1987 – a gesture of positive encouragement on the part of the state.[22] The law allowed both joint and wholly
owned foreign ventures. In March 1989 a single body, the State Committee on Cooperation and Investment (SCCI), was set up to oversee
foreign investment. It allowed foreigners to hold management posts and
repatriation of profits. The legislation identified several priority areas for
investment, including infrastructure projects, high-technology industries,
export production, ship repair, tourism and foreign-currency-earning
services. The rougher edges of the legislation were ironed out in early
1989 as Hanoi sought to ensure a more comprehensive investment infrastructure.

One feature of the legislation is that it gives preferential treatment to
overseas Vietnamese investors. Of the first 48 investment licences
granted in the nine months from June 1988, eleven were to overseas
Vietnamese.[23] The hope was that they would play a similar role in economic development to that of the overseas Chinese in China's moderniza-
tion process. In particular, it is hoped that their scientific and technical
expertise will be a significant factor in increasing economic efficiency.[24]
The number of projects involving overseas Vietnamese investment doubled in 1989, and the following year a further eleven projects, worth
$23.9 million, were licensed by the authorities. Most overseas Vietnam-
ese, however, especially the nearly one million in the United States,
remain hostile.[25]

Another important factor in the reform process from 1988 has been
the liberalization of trade. The decentralization of trade functions has
spawned new types of trade organizations in Vietnam. As in China, there
has been a growth of import-export corporations at the local level.
Liberalization of trade policy brought some early results, particularly
with regard to agricultural exports. Vietnam re-emerged as the world's
third largest rice exporter, behind Thailand and the United States. In
1989 it exported 1.4 million tonnes of rice, earning roughly $315 million,
nearly 20% of the country's total foreign exchange earnings.[26] Although
not so high in the following two years, rice exports continue to play a
significant role in the country's economic fortunes. Coffee cultivation,
which accounted for 90,000 hectares in 1980, all in state hands, had more
than doubled by the end of 1988, to 190,000 hectares, of which only 8%
was in state hands.

Despite a pre-industrial structure, inadequate institutions, stifling
bureaucracy and a shortage of qualified personnel, foreign investment
from the West also began to trickle into Vietnam in early 1989. By the

end of June 1989, 62 foreign investment projects had been approved, involving a total capital commitment of almost $640 million. Five projects accounted for 75% of the foreign funds, all in offshore oil and gas exploration. The contracts were signed by European heavyweights such as BP, Shell, Enterprise Oil, Total and Petrofina, as well as India's Oil and Natural Gas Commission. An Australian company, Overseas Telecommunications Corporation, won a major contract for developing and managing Vietnam's ailing telecommunications industry. The British marketing and services company, Inchcape, was among the first foreign trading companies to set up in Vietnam in May 1989. Interest was also rising in ASEAN countries. In the same month an official Thai trade delegation visited Vietnam, the first to do so in thirty years.[27]

The end of central planning

In 1989 the government effectively removed the last vestiges of central planning. It did so first of all, as a United Nations report noted, by 'openly and unambiguously committing itself to tackling monetary and fiscal problems'.[28] Whereas the mechanism for allocating resources hitherto had been the plan, it was henceforth to be the market. Autonomy of economic agents was to become a reality rather than a slogan as in the earlier reform experiments. The decision-making of producers and consumers was to be governed now by market-determined wages, prices, interest rates and foreign exchange rates. In early 1989 a drastic devaluation of the dong was undertaken, bringing it to levels close to the parallel market rate. Soon after, prices were substantially decontrolled, and by the end of the year only the prices for electricity, petrol and transport were still centrally controlled. Inflation had been reduced from triple-digit figures to a monthly rate of 2.8%.

The decision to implement a policy centred on real interest rates and a devaluation of the currency reduced the standing of the unofficial exchange market. In the past three years the gap between the official rate of the dong and the rate available on the black market has become almost negligible. Prior to 1989 a system of multiple exchange rates for different types of transactions was in operation. These different rates did not reflect a true exchange value, since they were not based on an analysis of prices or production costs, and the parallel exchange market was well placed to take advantage of the resultant distortions. The implementation of a unified exchange rate has allowed more flexibility in taking into account market forces.

Fiscal adjustment and enterprise restructuring were crucial to the success of the renovation process. The IMF considered the Vietnamese reforms an exemplary effort at economic stabilization and structural adjustment, and expressed disappointment that the United States and Japan seemed prepared to continue to block the country's re-entry into the international economic community.[29] Real interest rates had the effect of absorbing much of the parallel financial market into the banking structures. The reforms were an attempt to make a clear separation between the activities of the commercial banking sector and those of the central banking authorities. The central bank's inability to implement state plans to control the amount of credit and money available in the economy had been a major cause of hyperinflation. By passing all commercial banking functions to specialized banks, the emphasis has been put on creating an effective monetary management role for the state bank.

Until 1989 the core of the traditional central planning model was still intact. The abolition of the 'two-price' system ended the residual central planning functions of the state, and foreign trade was greatly liberalized. With the opening of the borders, goods flooded into Vietnam, and to all intents and purposes the government abandoned centralized control over international economic relations. Indeed, in many areas of the economy, the government had abandoned all pretence at control.

Taking stock in 1992
Vietnam's progress in the area of economic reform has, under the circumstances, been quite an achievement. To carry out an ambitious reform programme while denied access to the benefits deriving from membership of the world economic community is a feat that leads one to consider what Vietnam might be able to achieve were the economic embargo no longer in place. However, though substantial progress has been made towards establishing a base on which to build a modern market economy, *doi moi*'s successes to date should not mislead us into thinking that the Vietnamese economy has entered a prolonged period of stability. The enormous political fallout aside, the break-up of Vietnam's patron, the Soviet Union, poses further acute problems for Vietnam. Moscow's initial decision in 1990 to restructure its economic relations with all remaining communist party states had already placed Hanoi in difficulties. The subsequent dramatic collapse of communist party power in the Soviet Union exacerbated shortages, forcing Vietnam to buy oil and fertilizers, for example, on the international market.

Developments in the former Soviet Union following the failure of the August coup appear to have rendered virtually obsolete the economic cooperation agreements signed by Moscow and Hanoi in January 1991. This change in the economic relationship between Moscow and Hanoi, coming as it did hard on the heels of the decision of the former Soviet bloc countries in Eastern Europe to scrap Comecon, created an immediate shortfall in vital supplies of fuel, cotton, steel and fertilizer. The January 1991 agreements brought to a close an era in economic relations between the two countries, during which Vietnam was the beneficiary of extensive Soviet aid and assistance. Vietnam now finds itself with a huge debt to the Commonwealth of Independent States, believed to be around $15 billion, most of it owed to Russia. Not surprisingly, the Vietnamese are unhappy with a conversion of rouble debt into hard currency that arrives at anything like this figure, but can do little about it. Moscow seems aware that it is unlikely to be able to collect on the debt for some time to come. Vietnam now finds itself in a worse predicament than could have been anticipated even when the agreements were signed at the beginning of 1991. As new economic and political structures emerge within the old Soviet Union, it remains unclear what further impact these will have on Vietnamese economic relations with Russia and the other newly independent republics.

Although information to facilitate an accurate assessment is not readily available, cutbacks in supplies would appear to have already taken a toll on economic performance. Significant reductions in fuel and fertilizer supplies are particularly damaging to the economy, given that up to 1989 most of Vietnam's fuel and 80% of its fertilizer requirements came from the Soviet Union. In 1990, however, supplies were reduced to the extent that the Soviet Union was providing under two-thirds of Vietnam's fuel needs and only around half of its fertilizer requirements. The visit of party leader Nguyen Van Linh to Moscow in May 1991 failed to secure better terms or a guarantee of increased Soviet supplies. The figures for 1991 are expected to show another significant reduction. Trade with Moscow for the first six months of 1991 was only 15% of its 1990 level, with a particularly sharp drop in imports. However, Vietnam's exports (worth $715 million and 169 million roubles in the first half of the year) have so far held up quite well, largely due to a sharp rise in crude oil sales to Japan and an increase in exports of rubber, coffee and seafood.[30] In addition to the effect on industrial growth, where the rise in oil production is seen to cover falling output elsewhere in industry, agricultural growth rates may well suffer from fertilizer shortages.

The problems presented by the collapse of the Soviet Union, and the loss of markets there and in Eastern Europe, by no means constitute Vietnam's only economic difficulties. (Indeed, in the long run the collapse of the Soviet Union will be a blessing in disguise for the Vietnamese economy.) The return of inflation, mounting unemployment, smuggling, corruption and the continuing American embargo also threaten recent progress. Even foreign investment, one of the bright signs in the economy, has suffered from sluggish implementation and poor infrastructure.

Inflation has been a perennial problem of the modern Vietnamese economy. Until 1988 it had dogged attempts to achieve sustained growth and, although there was a considerable respite in the following years, it returned in 1991 to undermine confidence in the financial and banking systems. It still has a long way to go before it reaches the astronomical levels of 1986 and 1987, when the price index rose by 600% and 400% respectively, but it is nevertheless registering a disquieting upward trend. By January 1991 the monthly rate was up to 13.2% and, although this had fallen to 1.7% in June, it picked up again in the last half of the year. The price of food grains, as well as the rapid appreciation of gold and the dollar, all helped to fuel inflation. Increased demand for gold and foreign currency put pressure on the dong and led to its substantial devaluation in 1991. By the end of the year inflation was running at an annual rate of 75%.[31]

Rising inflation has led to a further increase in what is already an ominously high level of unemployment. A rapidly growing population, rising at an alarming rate of 2.3% per year, and the ending of subsidies to the state sector, have greatly aggravated the situation. In the two years ending in December 1990, more than 550,000 workers in the state sector lost their jobs. By August 1991 that figure was thought to have risen to a million. In addition, some half a million soldiers have been demobilized since the military withdrawal from Cambodia in September 1989, and the problem has been exacerbated by the return of 150,000 workers from Eastern Europe and the Middle East in 1990-91 and by about 13,000 boat-people from Hong Kong and elsewhere in Southeast Asia. More Vietnamese are likely to return home in 1992.[32]

Unemployment is particularly marked in urban areas and presents considerable potential for crime and social unrest, especially as some 90% of the unemployed are estimated to be in the 15–30 age group. The 1989 census found unemployment overall at 5.1%, but in the cities it was 12.3%. In 1990 unemployment in the largest urban area, Ho Chi Minh

City, was officially estimated at 230,000, but an estimate made by local economists in November 1991 put the figure at more than 500,000. The authorities have been able to do little to deal with the situation and have pinned their hopes instead on the private sector being able to offer jobs.[33]

The reform programme has also worsened the problems of smuggling and corruption, although, admittedly, with the exception of Singapore, these problems are widespread in Southeast Asia. The army newspaper, *Quan Doi Nhan Dan*, estimated in August 1990 that 60% of the goods entering the country do so without proper taxes.[34] The Cambodian settlement and the opening of the frontier with China have aggravated these problems further. A government commission found that $150 million worth of goods were smuggled into the country in 1990, almost certainly an underestimate.[35] The problem underlined the laxity and corruption among security forces and the weakening government control.

Smuggling, of course, is closely linked to the phenomenon of corruption, which has also blossomed in recent years. The trade union newspaper, *Lao Dong*, estimated in October 1991 that corruption had cost the country more than $2 billion since June 1990. More than 20,000 officials were sentenced or disciplined during that period.[36] Such problems, as already noted, are widespread in developing countries experiencing rapid economic development and coincide with growing inequality. They present, however, a particular difficulty for a communist-ruled country like Vietnam, whose governing party has previously been committed to the espousal of an egalitarian ideology. In January 1992 Prime Minister Vo Van Kiet, in an interview with the party daily, *Nhan Dan*, warned of 'the confrontation between luxury and misery, between cities and country', and of the need 'to establish a new order of sharing'.[37] The social strains caused by these problems are bound to grow in the immediate future.

The government and the Communist Party nevertheless seem convinced that there is no course that Vietnam can chart other than the ruthless pursuit of *doi moi*. Economic renovation and the shift to a market economy are, the party acknowledges, the only hope of delivering an improvement in the living standards of the people. Although there has been undoubted progress in agriculture and in some parts of industry, substantial obstacles remain, the most formidable being the relative absence of capital. Obviously, in part this is due to the crippling American embargo, but it is also due to the inadequacy of the country's banking system. Almost all modern capital remains in the hands of state units. Bank credit is almost entirely concentrated upon the state sector, and it is still difficult for the infant private sector to borrow.

In these circumstances foreign investment is obviously critical for the Vietnamese economy. Vietnam has many attractions for the foreign investor: a domestic market of 67 million people, cheap and well-disciplined labour, and an abundance of natural resources. In addition to substantial deposits of anthracite, iron ore, bauxite, tin, lead and gold, it has considerable offshore oil deposits. By the end of 1991, foreign companies had promised to invest almost $3 billion, yet of this sum not much more than $600 million has so far actually been spent, reflecting continued widespread caution among foreign investors. The American embargo continues to deter many, and especially Japanese, investors. Vietnam's infrastructure remains among the most underdeveloped in the world, with grossly inadequate ports, railways and airports, as well as insufficient power supplies. Moreover, in spite of the reforms, Vietnam still lacks a coherent body of commercial law and its banking structure leaves much to be desired.[38]

Despite these shortcomings, foreign interest is growing. Vietnam's most immediate hope lies in its oil industry. Companies from some fifteen countries are currently engaged in offshore oil exploration, including most of the world's big companies, with the exception of the Americans. Britain's involvement in the oil industry has ensured its becoming a major investor in Vietnam. British Petroleum signed an initial contract with Petro Vietnam in February 1989, agreeing to invest $60 million to explore for oil and gas over a five-year period. BP, like other companies granted exploration rights, is expected to absorb all the costs and in effect to take all the risks of the operation at this stage. Contracts are based on a production-sharing model used in Indonesia. Foreign oil companies are allowed to recoup exploration costs by keeping a share of production, with the remainder divided between Vietnam and the company. If successful, BP will be expected to make further investments of capital and technology over the remaining twenty years of its contract.[39]

Despite the optimism generated by such contracts, only one oilfield is currently in production – the White Tiger field off the coast of southern Vietnam, exploited by a Russian/Vietnamese joint venture. Oil represents the vast majority of actual foreign investment in Vietnam and nearly 40% of intended investment. But without a refinery, Vietnam must still pay more to import oil products than it makes from its present oil exports.[40] If, however, plans go ahead for a $1 billion oil refinery to be built by Sumitomo near Ho Chi Minh City, this is likely to have a considerable impact on the economy. Nevertheless oil production was up by 46% in 1991, with a total output of four million tonnes.

At the end of 1991 Vietnam indicated that it would try to do more to improve the investment climate for foreigners. Officials expressed a willingness to sign agreements on investment protection and promotion, and pacts on avoidance of double taxation. In November the government announced an overhaul of the banking system, establishing four autonomous national banks. In January 1992 Prime Minister Kiet said that the government was considering simplifying investment procedures and developing special zones where foreign investors would enjoy easier employment regulations and tax advantages.[41] At the same time the government has been encouraging the small private sector, which is likely to receive a substantial boost with the privatization of many state enterprises in the coming year. In November the party central committee finally decided that remaining subsidies to state enterprises will be 'entirely scrapped'.[42] If fully implemented, and the government may have no choice, this is likely to lead to many factories simply going under. One economist in Hanoi estimated that 30% of factories were already 'on the verge of collapse'.[43] Generally speaking, the technological development and productivity of most state industries is lamentable.

In short, impressive though Vietnam's progress has been in the past five years, the economy remains fragile and beset with problems. There is, it is true, a resilience about the Vietnamese people that has seen them through decades of conflict and is all too obvious today among the informal traders on the streets of Hanoi and Ho Chi Minh City, as well as in the rice fields of the Mekong delta. The 'market economy' already exists. Nevertheless, if the country's structural problems are to be overcome, substantial international assistance is surely essential. The United Nations Development Programme has estimated that official aid disbursements of over $4 billion a year are needed over the next five years, compared with a current annual flow of little more than $150 million. Without these sums it is hard to see how the country's infrastructure can be developed, industry re-equipped and agricultural progress sustained.[44]

5

THE FOREIGN POLICY CONTEXT

Vietnam learns to live with its neighbours
In the last quarter of 1991 Vietnam radically reversed its foreign policy of the previous twelve years and in the course of a few weeks succeeded in repairing its relations with both China and ASEAN. At the same time there was a marked improvement in its relations with the European Community, and a modest improvement in its relations with the United States and Japan. The international isolation to which it had been condemned since the communist victory of 1975, and more especially since the December 1978 invasion of Cambodia, finally seemed to be breaking down.

By the end of the year Vietnam had readjusted its foreign policy so decisively that ideological factors seemed now to play little or no role in the considerations of the foreign ministry and the Politburo in Hanoi. In large part, Vietnam has been forced to make these adjustments as what Hanoi often called 'the foundation stones' of Vietnamese foreign policy - the intimate alliance with the Soviet Union and the 'special relationship' between the three countries of Indochina – collapsed around it. Even traditional security concerns, so marked in Vietnam's policy towards Cambodia, appeared to have been shelved. Hanoi's long-standing objections to the UN-brokered peace agreement on Cambodia were abandoned and, with the final signing in Paris in October 1991 of that accord, the way was clear for a rapid improvement in relations with the outside world and, in particular, ASEAN and China.

In October the Prime Minister, Vo Van Kiet, visited Thailand, Indonesia and Singapore, the first visit to the ASEAN countries by a Vietnamese Prime Minister since 1978. In the course of that visit Mr Kiet made it clear that Vietnam wished to accede to the Bali Treaty of 1976, as the first step to an eventual membership of ASEAN.[1] That visit was followed by the removal by ASEAN countries of remaining restrictions on trade and investment with Vietnam. In January 1992 Mr Kiet visited Malaysia, and in late February he visited the remaining ASEAN members – Brunei and the Philippines – underlining Vietnam's determination to enter a new era in its relations with its Southeast Asian neighbours.

The new approach to ASEAN was complemented by the normalization of relations with China. In November 1991 the Prime Minister accompanied the party General Secretary, Do Muoi, on a visit to Peking which set the seal on rapprochement with China. In the words of one former Vietnamese diplomat interviewed in Hanoi in November: 'For the first time we are relying on diplomacy to safeguard security. In the past it was only used as a crown to military victory.' As in Europe, the cold war finally seemed to have been laid to rest; and, with an international settlement of the Cambodian conflict in place, regional tensions in Southeast Asia were reduced to a lower level than at any time since the end of the Second World War.

There were also notable improvements in Vietnam's relations with western countries, with several European Community members committing modest sums of economic aid to Vietnam for the first time since 1978. In November the French Foreign Minister, Roland Dumas, visited Vietnam. He was followed in January 1992 by his Italian counterpart, Gianni de Michelis, and by a British Foreign Office Minister, Lord Caithness. A reciprocal high-level Vietnamese visit to EC countries is on the cards for the second half of 1992. Relations with Australia similarly underwent significant improvement, and a visit by the Trade Minister, Neil Blewett, in November 1991 signalled that Canberra now considered relations with Hanoi fully normalized. A resumption of bilateral aid had already been announced.[2]

More disappointingly for Vietnam, its endeavours to normalize relations with the United States, the chief problem in its foreign policy, remain stalled. A promising start to bilateral negotiations in 1990 was not fulfilled in the following year. On the contrary, US-Vietnam relations seemed trapped by the 'roadmap', or framework, for normalization announced by Washington in April 1991, which postponed full normalization until the holding of UN-supervised elections in Cambodia, not likely to take place now until May 1993.[3] As a result, Vietnam continued to be denied desperately needed lines of credit by all the international lending institutions, such as the World Bank, the International Monetary

Fund and the Asian Development Bank. The US embargo against Vietnam also prevented American companies investing in, or even trading with, Vietnam. And although there were increasing frustrations among Japanese businessmen that their government – alone among those of the advanced industrial countries – continued to follow the US embargo, they remained reluctant to invest on a substantial scale in Vietnam.[4]

Despite the absence of any breakthrough in relations with the United States, Vietnam could be reasonably satisfied at the beginning of 1992 that it was finally emerging from the international isolation it had long endured. The opening up of its economy as a result of *doi moi* and its newly found acceptance by its regional neighbours seemed to indicate that it would be only a matter of time before it again became a fully-fledged member of the international community.

Escaping the Cambodian vortex

This breakthrough in relations with the outside world had not been achieved without considerable cost to Vietnam. The domestic prerequisite for such a breakthrough had been in place ever since the Stalinist model of centralized economic planning had been abandoned at the 1986 party congress. But, with minor exceptions, this dramatic about-turn in domestic economic policy had failed to bring about any real improvement in the country's relations with the outside world. Even in the narrow economic sense, most of the foreign capital that entered the country after the adoption in January 1988 of a liberal foreign investment code came not from the major economic powers or from Vietnam's immediate neighbours, but from Taiwan and Hong Kong. The one exception to this was British and French investment in the oil and gas industries.

But a real breakout from the ghetto in which the outside world had long confined Vietnam could only take place once Hanoi had finally relinquished what Michael Leifer has described as its 'abiding security fixation' with Cambodia.[5] Despite its unilateral and unsupervised withdrawal of forces from Cambodia in September 1989, ending almost a decade-long involvement, Vietnam still hoped to retain a special relationship with the Phnom Penh government and refused to countenance any substantial change in the political status quo in Cambodia. Although this imposed appalling costs on Vietnam, in particular impeding the implementation of *doi moi* in the economic field, the leadership was unwilling to forgo the special relationship with Cambodia that it had fought so long to obtain.[6] Indeed, there were indications in early 1990 that Vietnamese military units were being brought back to be deployed in Cambodia on a short-term basis.[7]

In short, no matter how fundamental the domestic changes being implemented by Vietnam, its continued involvement in the Cambodian conflict still prevented its successful acceptance in the international economy. Vietnam was not prepared to abdicate its long-held positions of influence in Cambodia, or, for that matter, Laos. Notwithstanding the withdrawal of its forces from Laos in 1987–8 and its more public withdrawal from Cambodia in September 1989, as late as mid-1991 there were few indications that it was prepared to budge from this position. Vietnam continued to hope that its neighbours and the international community at large would at least accept a partial solution to the Cambodian conflict, thereby ending its international dimensions. However, no real advantage accrued to Vietnam from its troop withdrawal from Cambodia.

In large part this was because ASEAN, China and the United States were determined that there be a comprehensive political solution to the conflict, which entailed power-sharing between the warring Cambodian factions and the end of what were seen in many capitals as Vietnam's hegemonistic ambitions in Indochina. Also, the international situation had moved very much to its disadvantage. In particular, the strong support that it had received from the Soviet Union since the late 1970s, and which found expression in the 1978 treaty of friendship between the two countries, had effectively evaporated. In line with his 'new political thinking', President Gorbachev had terminated his own country's involvement in the Afghan conflict in February 1989 and had achieved a rapprochement with China in May that year. Moreover, following the failure of the August 1989 Paris peace conference on Cambodia, the Soviet Union played a full role with the other permanent members of the United Nations Security Council in the search for a durable solution to the Cambodian conflict.

In August 1990 the Permanent Five adopted a framework agreement for settling the conflict, which effectively terminated Soviet support for Vietnam's position. A secret summit between the Chinese and Vietnamese leaderships in Chengdu, China, in September 1990 failed to produce any substantial breakthrough that would reduce Hanoi's hopelessly isolated position. Until the spring of 1991, however, Vietnam continued to back its ally in Phnom Penh in opposing that plan, which it saw as fundamentally undermining its own security interests. It had an added incentive for doing so in that the UN plan envisaged the staging of multi-party elections on Vietnam's doorstep, an unpalatable move for Hanoi given the collapse of traditional Leninist political structures in Eastern Europe.

Nevertheless, the strategic environment in which Vietnam's ruling Communist Party found itself by early 1991 had deteriorated markedly. Its dogged refusal to contemplate a change in the political status quo in Cambodia was increasingly untenable. The decline in Soviet support has already been noted, and, in what turned out to be a final visit to the Soviet Union by party leader Nguyen Van Linh in May 1991, Hanoi found little support for its position.[8] Within months President Gorbachev was to find himself politically neutralized as a result of the failed August coup, and the Communist Party of the Soviet Union banned. Vietnam's security fixation with Cambodia had long acted as an impediment to the successful implementation of economic reform, but now the impasse over the Cambodian conflict threatened the very basis of Communist Party rule in Vietnam.

The collapse of communism in first Eastern Europe, and then the Soviet Union, and the abrupt termination of the Socialist Commonwealth, finally drove home to the leadership in Hanoi a fact that it had long sought to avoid: that it could no longer afford to escape a choice between its security needs and its economic needs. The future of continued party rule in Vietnam was inextricably entwined with the success of economic renovation. The leadership in Hanoi was acutely aware that the primary cause of the collapse of communism in Eastern Europe was the failure to produce a viable economic model. And, without a settlement of the Cambodian conflict, Vietnam could not expect acceptance by the international community. By finally accepting the UN peace plan, Vietnam was forced to acknowledge that the balance of power in Indochina has shifted to its disadvantage and, inevitably, to the advantage of its long-standing foe, China. Vietnam could no longer ignore the centrality of its relationship with China in its foreign policy. It was a price the leadership in Hanoi had to pay to guarantee not only the success of its economic reforms, but also by 1991 the Communist Party's continued exercise of political power. The contradiction that had long existed between domestic and foreign policy, between economic and strategic priorities, had been finally resolved.

As noted, the resolution of that conflict has permitted a radical and promising shift in Vietnam's foreign policy, one which holds the hope that it will finally be accepted into the international community. At the same time the changes in Vietnamese foreign policy may well usher in for Southeast Asia as a whole an unparalleled opportunity for regional peace and stability.

Clearly, the roots of Vietnam's international isolation in recent years, and what can only be described as the dismal failure of its foreign policy, can largely be ascribed to its 1978 invasion of Cambodia and its toppling from power of the infamous Khmer Rouge. However, it has to be said that relations with ASEAN, and even more so with China, were already cool before the military intervention in Cambodia. As has often been noted, at the heart of that conflict was a deeply felt concern by Vietnam for its own national security against a background of a centuries-old antagonism towards China.[9] For Hanoi, these fears were cruelly confirmed within weeks of the communist triumphs of April 1975, when the first border clashes occurred between the Khmer Rouge and Vietnam. While Vietnam had fought in recent times for its independence from France and the United States, its very identity as a nation had been forged in conflict with China. For almost a millennium after it had escaped China's embrace in the eleventh century, it continued to live in fear of Imperial China. And, although it had defeated France and the United States, it was only too aware that they were distant powers, whereas China was on the doorstep.

The key factor in transforming the relationship between the two countries was Vietnam's changing relationship with the Soviet Union. Throughout the bitter years of Sino-Soviet polemics in the 1960s, Vietnam had successfully resisted taking sides with either Moscow or Peking. Ho Chi Minh, in his deathbed testimony in 1969, had pleaded for a return to the unity of the communist world.[10] But while Vietnam was still fighting the Americans, neutrality between the Soviet Union and China was an option for Hanoi. Neither Moscow nor Peking wanted to be seen as failing to aid Vietnam, viewed by both as the epicentre of the struggle against American imperialism. President Nixon's historic 1972 visit to China began to change the picture.

Victory in 1975 forced Vietnam's leadership to think of postwar economic reconstruction. From the start it was clear that China, itself emerging from the tumult of the Cultural Revolution, was in no position to compete with the Soviet Union as Hanoi's main economic benefactor. Moreover, many in the leadership in Hanoi, led perhaps by Le Duan, saw Moscow as the real centre of world communism.[11] In the circumstances, the best Peking could hope to do was to try to minimize the influence of the Soviet Union over Hanoi, or encourage western countries to assist Vietnam. But the latter was never a viable proposition. Even before

Vietnam's 1978 invasion of Cambodia, few western countries, Sweden excepted, showed any inclination to render economic assistance to Vietnam for postwar reconstruction.

Economic necessity, compounded by Vietnam's tense relations with China's ally, the Khmer Rouge, effectively compelled Hanoi's leadership to turn to the Soviet Union. Vietnam's treatment of its own ethnic Chinese minority was another factor in its deteriorating relations with China. But if Vietnam had not moved closer to the Soviet Union, China would almost certainly have ignored the treatment of ethnic Chinese, since it had tolerated far worse treatment meted out by Pol Pot to ethnic Chinese in 'Democratic Kampuchea'. By early 1978, relations between the two allies – previously described by Peking 'as close as lips and teeth' – had reached breaking point. In June, Vietnam joined Comecon and in November signed a treaty of friendship with the Soviet Union. In China's parlance it had become the 'Cuba of Asia'.[12]

From that point on, conflict was virtually inevitable. Hanoi's full-scale invasion in December 1978 to topple the demonic Khmer Rouge from power in Cambodia prompted China in turn to attack Vietnam in February 1979. Vietnam's refusal to yield to Chinese pressure let loose long-simmering frustration in China at its inability to control its smaller southern neighbour. But China, having failed to control its neighbour by peaceful means, fared no better in using force. Thereafter relations between the two countries were to remain glacial until 1990, and then thawed only gradually.

The conflict that ensued in Cambodia throughout the 1980s was in many ways a proxy war between Vietnam and China. Unfortunately for Vietnam, despite the hideous record in power of the Khmer Rouge, few in the international community took Hanoi's side, and the UN judged the rights of states superior to the rights of individuals. In the atmosphere of the new cold war of the early 1980s, the West and ASEAN effectively took China's side, a move made politically more comfortable by the formation in June 1982 of the Coalition Government of Democratic Kampuchea, which brought together under one umbrella the Khmer Rouge, the non-communist Khmer People's National Liberation Front and the supporters of the former head of state, Prince Sihanouk. The impasse that prevailed thereafter was finally broken only in June 1991, when the warring Cambodian factions, including Hanoi's ally, the Phnom Penh government, accepted the full implementation of the UN peace plan for Cambodia.

Vietnam and the Soviet Union – end of an era

Just as Vietnam's relationship with the Soviet Union was the key factor in determining its relations with China in the late 1970s, so the collapse of the Moscow/Hanoi relationship in the late 1980s enabled a rapprochement between Vietnam and China. A study of Vietnamese foreign policy written in 1990 would probably have concluded that the country's most important external relationship was still that with the Soviet Union. But when the seventh congress of the Vietnamese Communist Party met in June 1991, party documents contained only passing references to relations with the Soviet Union, and the 'Political Programme' adopted at the congress contained none at all.[13] The proceedings reflected both the decline of the Soviet Union itself and the steady downgrading of relations that had been taking place between Moscow and Hanoi in the preceding years.[14] The new thinking in Soviet foreign policy towards Asia, reflected in President Gorbachev's speeches in Vladivostok in July 1986 and Krasnoyarsk in September 1988, served notice to Vietnam that the close relationship they had enjoyed since the treaty of friendship of 1978 was increasingly being brought into question. The rapprochement with China in 1989, as well as the Soviet Union's active participation with other permanent members of the Security Council in the search for peace in Cambodia, underlined the fact that Moscow no longer considered Vietnam a strategically important ally.[15]

At the same time, as noted in Chapter 4, Vietnam's economic relationship with the Soviet Union was undergoing considerable change. Traditionally one of the largest recipients of Soviet aid, with disbursements of $2 billion a year in the late 1980s, Vietnam saw this programme effectively terminated at the end of 1990. Moreover, from January 1991, trade between Vietnam and the former Soviet Union moved to a hard currency basis, ending the subsidizing of Soviet exports. Remarkably, given the continuing American embargo, Vietnam has weathered the potential crisis that this could have induced in its economy, although its foreign exchange reserves and unemployment levels have undoubtedly suffered.

The failure of the attempted putsch in Moscow in August 1991 and the subsequent collapse of the Soviet Union itself have undoubtedly been great political shocks for Vietnam's leadership. At a stroke, Vietnam has lost the ally that it has depended on economically, diplomatically and militarily for almost two decades. In the wake of the Soviet collapse, however, it has accelerated its own economic reforms and has made a promising start at improving relations with China and ASEAN. The dramatic events of late 1991 have probably also made a return to the orthodox communism of the past as impossible for Vietnam as it is for the Soviet Union.

As 1992 began, Vietnam was searching for a new relationship with the Commonwealth of Independent States. A delegation led by Deputy Foreign Minister Nguyen Dy Nien visited Russia and several other republics at the end of January. Vietnam has already said that it is willing to establish diplomatic relations with the constituent republics of the CIS.[16] But little remains of the formerly close relationship, except – in Vietnam's case – a considerable foreign debt. As for the future, it is difficult to foresee any substantial relationship between Vietnam and either Russia or the CIS.

Vietnam and Cambodia – a new start

The acceptance by all four Cambodian factions of the UN peace plan and the deployment in March 1992 of UNTAC (the United Nations Transitional Authority in Cambodia) offer for the first time in decades the possibility of a new relationship between Vietnam and Cambodia.[17] Despite the fact that the UN plan inevitably has entailed changes to the political and military status quo in Cambodia, it should in the long run offer safeguards for Vietnam's legitimate security concerns. Reluctantly, by the middle of 1991, Vietnam seemed prepared to accept the inevitability that meaningful economic reform could never be implemented as long as it was still shunned by most of the international community.

Already at the seventh party congress in June references to Cambodia were notably low key compared with previous congresses. Thus, whereas the Political Report of the sixth congress in 1986 spoke of the special friendship between the peoples of Indochina being 'a sacred international duty and a task of strategic importance', the Political Report in 1991 spoke only of the 'special friendship and solidarity between the party and people of Vietnam and the parties and peoples of Laos and Cambodia [having] constantly developed'.[18] Moreover, the Political Programme adopted at that congress identifies the foreign policy objective of the party as being 'to constantly consolidate and develop the traditional relations of friendship and cooperation with other socialist countries, and with the neighbouring countries of Indochina' – a formulation which would appear to countenance the possibility that Laos and Cambodia are no longer socialist.[19] Two months later, in a further sign of Vietnam's retreat over Cambodia, Deputy Foreign Minister Nguyen Dy Nien met with Prince Sihanouk, the head of the Supreme National

Council and long-time leader of the anti-Vietnamese resistance, and formally invited him to visit Vietnam at the end of the year.[20]

But if Vietnam accepted the implementation of the UN peace plan and the return of Prince Sihanouk from his thirteen years of exile, a far more difficult pill for it to swallow was the formal abandonment by the ruling party in Phnom Penh in October of Marxism-Leninism, and its acceptance of pluralism and a free market economy.[21] The move came at a special congress of the Vietnamese-tutored Khmer People's Revolutionary Party (KPRP), which changed its name to the Cambodian People's Party and dropped its long-standing pro-Vietnamese leader, Heng Samrin, in favour of the more nationalistic Chea Sim. The congress made no mention of either the party's or the country's relationship with Vietnam. No Vietnamese delegate had been invited to the congress and, in an evident expression of concern, Hanoi sent a Politburo member, Nguyen Duc Binh, to Phnom Penh in late October. At the end of the visit Binh was quoted by the Cambodian News Agency as having 'expressed the firm support of the Vietnamese Communist Party for the Cambodian People's Party platform'.[22] Two weeks later Vietnam symbolically removed from Phnom Penh its veteran ambassador, Ngo Dien, who had served since 1980 and been regarded in many quarters as a Vietnamese proconsul.[23]

These events confirmed that Vietnam's much-vaunted 'special relationship' with Cambodia was at an end. In return for effectively terminating that relationship, it had achieved its long-sought rapprochement with China in November 1991 and improved its relations with ASEAN and most western countries, although not the United States. With many bilateral issues outstanding, such as the question of the Vietnamese minority in Cambodia and the demarcation of their mutual border, Vietnam now has a stronger interest than most countries in seeing the UN peace accord work. The postponement of the visit to Vietnam by Prince Sihanouk, originally scheduled for late 1991, must increase Hanoi's anxieties about its future relationship with a more nationalist government in Cambodia.

Vietnam and China: as close as lips and teeth?

The acceptance by Vietnam and its ally, the Phnom Penh government, of the UN peace agreement enabled Hanoi and Peking to normalize their relations. It was a rapprochement urgently sought by Vietnam, and to a lesser extent by China, in the wake of the Soviet Union's collapse and

Vietnam's failure to bring about a normalization of relations with the United States. As one of the architects of China's Indochina policy, Deputy Foreign Minister Han Nianlong, had predicted in 1979, 'It is only when the Soviets can no longer support the Vietnamese that a political solution to the crisis will be possible.'[24]

The road to Peking was a long and hard one for Vietnam, and even now relations can only be characterized as proper, rather than warm. Relations between the two countries had been deteriorating since the early 1970s, when China moved to normalize its relations with the United States at a time when US forces were still fighting in Vietnam. After 1975, their already cool relations worsened as Vietnam took tough measures against its ethnic Chinese minority, moved closer to the Soviet Union and finally, in December 1978, invaded Cambodia, toppling the Khmer Rouge, whom China had clearly seen as a useful bulwark against Vietnamese expansionism. China retaliated by launching a punitive attack against northern Vietnam in February 1979 and by giving strong military and diplomatic backing to the anti-Vietnamese forces in Cambodia.[25] Thereafter, by virtue of their proxy war in Cambodia and Vietnam's close relationship with the Soviet Union, Peking and Hanoi remained at daggers drawn until the late 1980s. Whereas, from 1986 on, Vietnam showed an obvious interest in seeking to improve relations with China, the leadership in Peking, having lost considerable face in 1978–9 and having invested so heavily in the Cambodian conflict, was determined not to let Hanoi off the hook. Even at the end, Peking made it clear that an official summit could take place only after the signing of the Paris peace treaty on Cambodia. Vietnam had to be forced to admit that its attempt at exercising political hegemony over Indochina had failed. In the end, the terms Vietnam had to accept for rapprochement were not very different from those demanded by Han Nianlong in talks in Hanoi in April 1979.[26]

By the end of the 1980s it was clear to the leadership in Hanoi that its gamble that the *de facto* alliance forged between China and ASEAN would not last had not worked. Moreover, it was increasingly obvious that China would not allow a comprehensive diplomatic settlement that allowed Vietnam to get away with its 'special relationship' intact. China had the patience, the determination and the resources, as well as the international friends, to play a long-term game. Vietnam had not. And, for Vietnam, the Chinese, unlike the French or the Americans, will always be there. Measures by the Vietnamese to reduce tensions along their border with China in 1987, and even the unilateral withdrawal of their forces from Cambodia in September 1989, still did not meet with any substantive response from China. Although low-level talks between the two countries had resumed in January 1989, as late as June 1990 the Chinese Deputy Foreign Minister, Xu Dunxin, was describing the two sides as remaining as far apart as ever. A secret summit between the two countries in Chengdu in September 1990, soon after the United States announced that it was reviewing its relations with Vietnam, led to a tentative agreement on Cambodia, but failed to lead to any major break-through.[27]

In the course of 1991, however, a perceptible thaw set in. Vietnamese sources attest that the deepening crisis in the Soviet Union and the US victory in the Gulf war played an important role in China taking a more conciliatory line towards Vietnam.[28] For its part, China was increasingly anxious to see the Cambodia issue resolved as it sought for the first time since 1949 to normalize relations with all the countries of Southeast Asia. In 1990, Peking had established diplomatic relations with Indonesia and Singapore. Continuing hostility towards Vietnam was increasingly out of step with China's desire to be accepted throughout Southeast Asia. In July, in a sign of its changing attitude, Peking hosted a meeting of the Cambodian Supreme National Council, inviting to China for the first time the Prime Minister of the Phnom Penh government, Hun Sen. At the end of that month General Le Duc Anh, the second-ranking Vietnamese Politburo member, made a secret trip to Peking, which paved the way for full normalization. The final details were settled in a visit by Vietnamese Foreign Minister Nguyen Manh Cam in early September.[29]

The visit of General Secretary Do Muoi and Prime Minister Vo Van Kiet in November set the seal on the new relationship. At Chinese insistence, possibly to allay ASEAN fears, stress was laid on the normalization of state-to-state relations, as opposed to party relations. The visit was described as 'high-ranking', but not as a party and government summit, as it would have been in the past.[30] The timing of the visit demonstrated only too well who had won the contest. By signing the Cambodian accord in Paris only two weeks earlier, Vietnam had fulfilled the condition that China had imposed more than a decade before as a prelude to the normalization of relations.

Quite apart from the obvious security benefits, the economic advantages that will accrue to Vietnam from the normalization of relations with China will be substantial. This is especially the case for the poorer northern half of the country, which has benefited far less from foreign investment than the South. There is a complementarity between northern Vietnam and the neighbouring Chinese provinces of Yunnan and Guangxi, which promises rich rewards for both countries in the future.

Nevertheless, despite the settlement of the Cambodia question, normalization of relations has left a host of bilateral problems. The most obvious are the two countries' ill-defined borders and their competing claims of sovereignty over the Paracel and Spratly Islands, which have caused considerable friction in the past. In addition, Peking is known to have raised objections to the role Taiwan is playing in the Vietnamese economy, where it is the largest foreign investor, and has demanded that up to 250,000 Vietnamese Chinese expelled in 1977–8 be allowed to return. China is further requesting the repayment of debts going back to the 1960s. This comprehensive list will prevent the two countries being 'as close as lips and teeth' for many years to come. Just as rapprochement between the Soviet Union and China in 1989 did not mean a return to the honeymoon period of the 1950s, relations between Vietnam and China are unlikely for the foreseeable future to recapture their past closeness. On all the outstanding issues between the two countries, Vietnam is in a weak negotiating position, and its current political weakness was underlined by the visits of party and military delegations to Peking in March 1992.[31] In short, good relations with China are vital for Vietnam given the collapse of the Soviet Union and the absence of relations with the United States.

Vietnam and ASEAN: coming into the fold

Although Vietnam's relations with its ASEAN neighbours have never been as bitter and acrimonious as Sino-Vietnamese relations, they have nevertheless been paralysed for the past thirteen years by the Cambodian conflict. Even before Vietnam's invasion of Cambodia, relations were cool, although Hanoi had made some attempt after 1976 to improve them. The communist victory in April 1975 had been a rude shock to ASEAN governments, many of which, especially Thailand and the Philippines, were struggling to cope with communist insurgencies of their own.[32] For its part, Vietnam viewed ASEAN with suspicion, refusing to acknowledge it as a regional entity. For the Politburo in Hanoi, ASEAN was a relic of the past, differing in nature little from a military alliance like SEATO (Southeast Asia Treaty Organization). A tour of ASEAN countries by the Vietnamese Prime Minister, Pham Van Dong, in September–October 1978 did little to allay mutual suspicions, particularly as

71

that visit was followed within a few months by Vietnam's invasion of Cambodia.[33]

Indeed, that invasion confirmed ASEAN's worst suspicions about Vietnam and effectively drove the association into a united front with China on the Cambodian question. Almost overnight one of the world's largest armies had arrived on ASEAN's doorstep. Inevitably, fears about Vietnam's long-term intentions in Southeast Asia were greatest in Thailand, the only ASEAN state that shared borders with communist Indochina. Quite apart from the ideological threat that many ASEAN governments still perceived as emanating from Hanoi, for Thailand in particular the Vietnamese invasion of Cambodia seemed to be a reversion to traditional pre-colonial patterns of conflict in Southeast Asia. Vietnam's insistence on a 'special relationship' among the peoples of Indochina seemed all too reminiscent to Thailand of the attempts of the Nguyen dynasty in the nineteenth century to establish Vietnamese hegemony over Laos and Cambodia.[34] Thailand responded by allowing China to re-equip the Khmer Rouge through its territory.

In its perception of the Vietnamese threat, Thailand received strong backing from Singapore. Other ASEAN members, such as Malaysia and, to an even greater extent, Indonesia, saw China as a greater threat to Southeast Asia than Vietnam. Yet, despite Vietnamese attempts throughout the 1980s to play upon differences within the association, ASEAN retained an impressive unity in opposition to the Vietnamese intervention in Cambodia. Indonesia played a unique role within ASEAN by keeping open lines of communication with Vietnam and by searching for ways to open peace negotiations. But President Suharto made it clear that Indonesia valued its role within ASEAN and would not sacrifice the organization on the altar of a peace settlement. To Vietnam's disappointment, ASEAN's cohesion withstood the test posed by Hanoi's intervention in Cambodia. Indeed, ASEAN's standing in the world community grew substantively through the 1980s as a result of its political and diplomatic solidarity over the Cambodian question. Essentially, its political goals throughout the decade after the Vietnamese invasion have been achieved, namely a withdrawal of Vietnamese forces under international supervision and the holding of free elections under UN auspices.

The reversal of the 1979 invasion has left ASEAN in a strong position in its dealings with Vietnam. As the outlines of a political settlement in Cambodia took shape in the late 1980s, in no small part because of ASEAN's efforts, so Vietnam's attitude to the association also underwent change. Despite continued differences over the content and form of such a settlement, Vietnam increasingly saw that its future lay as a member of the Southeast Asian community, rather than as a member of the ailing Soviet bloc. Some ASEAN members, notably Indonesia and Malaysia, openly welcomed this possibility. Even before the signing of the Paris peace treaty on Cambodia, Indonesia had effectively taken the lead in fully normalizing relations when President Suharto became the first ASEAN head of state to visit Vietnam in November 1990. In a joint communiqué at the end of the visit, Vietnam reiterated its hope of joining ASEAN.[35]

Since the seventh party congress in June 1991, Vietnam has stressed its desire to expand ties with all nations. As noted above, Prime Minister Vo Van Kiet has now visited all six ASEAN members – Brunei, Indonesia, Malaysia, the Philippines, Singapore and Thailand. Before he visited Indonesia in October 1991, Vietnam sent a letter to the standing committee of the association expressing its interest in acceding to the 1976 Bali Treaty on Amity and Cooperation, which pledges signatories to rely exclusively on peaceful processes in the settlement of intra-regional disputes.[36] Ironically, the ASEAN heads of government had drawn up this treaty in 1976 to act as a political bridge between the association and Vietnam. It had taken Vietnam fifteen years to indicate its willingness to cross that bridge. The *modus vivendi* that ASEAN hoped to encourage by the Bali Treaty had finally been achieved.

In perhaps the most significant stop on that tour, Singapore, the Vietnamese premier spoke of Vietnam's desire to work for a 'new order' in Southeast Asia. For his part, Singapore's Prime Minister, Goh Chok Tong, expressed support for Vietnam's bid to accede to the Bali Treaty. The two countries also agreed to exchange diplomatic missions and to establish direct air links. Singapore made it clear during the visit that it considered that there were no bilateral problems remaining between the two countries now that a political settlement had been concluded in Cambodia. By the end of 1991, Singapore had emerged as Vietnam's second-largest trading partner after Japan; and, in November, it lifted its ban on investment in Vietnam. This was a significant gesture, given the leading role the island republic has played within ASEAN in formulating policy over Cambodia, and its long-standing suspicion of Vietnamese communism. Perhaps the most extraordinary development of the visit, and a powerful indication of the dramatically changed circumstances in the region, was the reported request by Kiet to the former Singapore Prime Minister and staunch anticommunist, Lee Kuan Yew, informally to advise the Vietnamese authorities on economic reform.[37]

There is little doubt that the success of Mr Kiet's visit will prove a landmark in Vietnam's relations with ASEAN. It is now widely expected that the ASEAN foreign ministers, at their annual meeting in July 1992, will accept the formal accession of Vietnam to the Bali Treaty. Thereafter Vietnam could look forward to observer status in ASEAN, on a similar basis to that enjoyed by Papua New Guinea. But Vietnam is too important a country in Southeast Asia to be outside ASEAN forever. Sooner or later Hanoi and the member states of the association will have to decide how close their relationship is going to be. For Vietnam, the advantages of eventually joining would appear far to outweigh any disadvantages. Not least, membership of ASEAN might permit Vietnam to manage its relations with outside powers like China and the United States better than it has in the past. Within ASEAN there is undoubtedly residual unease by virtue of the fact that Vietnam remains a communist-governed state. At the minimum, ASEAN will want to wait some years to see whether Vietnam's embrace of the free market is a marriage of convenience or whether it marks a fundamental commitment to market capitalism.

However, it is important to remember that while ASEAN can feel satisfied with the resolution of the Cambodian conflict, bilateral problems remain between Vietnam and one member state, Thailand. These include the question of Vietnamese settlers in northeast Thailand, alleged Thai support for right-wing Vietnamese groups, fishing disputes and unresolved claims to overlapping economic zones at sea. Behind these problems lies the centuries-old antipathy between Vietnam and Thailand, reinforced by the history of the past four decades, when Bangkok supported the American war in Indochina and, more recently, the Cambodian guerrillas.[38]

Despite these differences, Thailand has everything to gain from better relations with Vietnam, especially in the economic sphere, where Bangkok has long nurtured ambitions to turn Indochina into a marketplace and source of raw materials for Thailand's booming economy. Separate visits in January by the commander of the Thai armed forces, General Suchinda Kraprayoon, and the Prime Minister Anand Panyarachun, the first by a Thai head of government, indicated the desire to solve bilateral problems and even contained the extraordinary suggestion from General Suchinda of military cooperation.[39] Significantly, Thailand has also now called for the lifting of the American trade embargo against Vietnam.[40] For its part, Vietnam has welcomed closer relations with Thailand after decades of hostility, but Hanoi has been careful to encourage close economic links with Singapore as a balance to economic dependence on Thailand.

Vietnam and the West

The European Community

Like ASEAN, the countries of the European Community have moved swiftly to adjust their policies towards Vietnam in the light of the political settlement over Cambodia. Indeed, even before the signing of the Paris peace treaty, several European countries had acknowledged the progress Vietnam had made in terms of economic reform. As well as improving their bilateral relations with Vietnam, EC countries have expressed concern to the United States at what they see as the futility of its embargo against Vietnam. In addition, Vietnam has formal relations with the European Community as a whole, as well as with individual members. Several EC members, notably France and Italy, have also supported an initiative designed to break the logjam denying Vietnam credits from the IMF and the World Bank.[41]

Unlike the United States, most EC members, including the UK, France, Germany and Italy, have had long-standing diplomatic relations with Vietnam. After 1975, their previous recognition of the Democratic Republic of Vietnam (North Vietnam) was extended to the Socialist Republic of Vietnam that was proclaimed following reunification. However, after Vietnam's invasion of Cambodia in December 1978, relations between EC members and Vietnam deteriorated. Existing programmes of economic aid, which were anyway modest, were curtailed. Indeed, the only West European country to maintain an aid programme after the invasion of Cambodia was a non-EC member, Sweden. By 1990 that aid programme amounted to $50 million a year.

Although EC countries gave firm public backing to ASEAN's stance on Cambodia, reflecting the close relations the two regional associations enjoy, several European governments were privately concerned at a policy that they saw as isolating Vietnam and making it more dependent on the Soviet Union. Moreover, public opinion in western Europe was unhappy at a policy that gave support to a resistance coalition in Cambodia which included the infamous Khmer Rouge. France, in particular, tried to use its good offices to mediate between the parties to the Cambodia conflict. In December 1987 it played host to the first meeting between Prince Sihanouk and Hun Sen, the Prime Minister of the Phnom Penh government. Two years later it helped to organize the abortive Paris peace conference on Cambodia in August 1989. Thereafter, France and Great Britain, as permanent members of the UN Security Council, played a critical role in drafting the UN peace agreement for Cambodia. Since the other three permanent members – China, the Soviet Union and the United States – had all been closely involved in the Cambodian conflict, France and Britain had to bridge the differences between the external parties to the conflict and help find an agreement that was acceptable to ASEAN, Vietnam and the warring Cambodian factions themselves.

Since the signing of the 1991 Paris peace treaty, all the major EC countries have sent high-level delegations to Vietnam, reflecting their desire to see that country fully integrated again into the international community. The French Foreign Minister, Roland Dumas, visited Vietnam in late November and announced that France would double its economic aid in 1992 to FFr 95 million ($17.3 million). He also said that France would propose Vietnam as the host of the 1995 francophone summit.[42] Days before M. Dumas's visit, the German Minister for Economic Cooperation, Hans-Peter Repnik, pledged on a visit to Hanoi that Germany would give Vietnam $17 million in aid in 1992. It should be noted, however, that this is far short of the $40 million aid donated by the former East German government in the firs nine months of 1990 alone. In January 1992 the Italian Foreign Minister, Gianni de Michelis, visited Vietnam and announced that his country, too, would be increasing its foreign aid programme in the coming year.

Despite these promising developments in EC/Vietnam relations, a number of outstanding problems remain. There is concern in several EC countries about the human rights situation in Vietnam, and this was raised forcefully by M. Dumas during his visit in November 1991. For Germany and for Britain, with respect to Hong Kong, there is also the vexed question of the repatriation of Vietnamese who do not qualify as refugees. Many thousands of Vietnamese worked in East Germany before its collapse, and 8,500 more arrived there in 1991 from other East European countries. Some 60,000 Vietnamese are currently living in Germany, of whom at least 20,000 are there illegally. In January 1992 the German government signed an agreement with the Vietnamese authorities under the terms of which some 15,000 Vietnamese are expected to return home.[43]

Bilateral relations between the United Kingdom and Vietnam have been similarly preoccupied in recent years with this issue, as a political solution to the Cambodian conflict has taken shape. As economic conditions deteriorated in Vietnam in the mid-1980s, a continuing flood of boat-people arrived on the shores of Southeast Asia. When the ASEAN countries closed the doors on new arrivals, Hong Kong became the favoured choice of many boats leaving Vietnam, especially from the northern half of the country. Indeed, by 1991, Hong Kong was receiving

95% of the new arrivals in the region. For the desperately overcrowded British colony, the problem became acute and led, in June 1988, to the authorities introducing 'screening' to separate genuine refugees from economic migrants. The vast majority of the arrivals have been deemed to be economic migrants, and a policy of voluntary, and later forced, repatriation has been introduced to return them to Vietnam. The British government and the EC have given funds for their necessary reintegration into Vietnamese society.

The issue has tended to preoccupy ministerial visits to Vietnam. In April 1989, Lord Glenarthur, a British Foreign Office Minister, became the first British minister to visit the country since the communist takeover in the South in 1975. In February 1990, he was followed by his successor, Mr Francis Maude. Although willing to accept back voluntary repatriates – 13,000 returned from Hong Kong between 1989 and 1991 – the Vietnamese government was reluctant until late 1991 to receive those forcibly returned, in large part for fear of further worsening its relations with the United States, which has voiced strong opposition to the idea. In October 1991 the Vietnamese, British and Hong Kong governments reached agreement on an Orderly Repatriation Programme to resettle those boat-people in Hong Kong camps deemed not to be refugees.[44] Vietnam has also said that it is willing to take back boat- people from ASEAN countries who do not qualify for refugee status.

In January, Lord Caithness, the British Foreign Office Minister responsible for Asia and the Pacific, visited Vietnam for further talks on the issue. Following a meeting with Vo Van Kiet, who expressed his appreciation at the resolution of the boat-people issue, Lord Caithness said that Britain would now press the United States to lift its embargo against Vietnam.[45] Some 60,000 Vietnamese remain in camps in Hong Kong, the vast majority of whom are not deemed to be refugees.

But there is still much more that could be done to develop EC/ Vietnamese relations. Aid from western Europe, on a bilateral or an EC level, remains exceptionally modest. Moreover, Vietnamese exports to Europe still face stiff EC restrictions. For example, whereas Vietnam formerly exported 300 million textile pieces annually to the Soviet Union, the EC restricts it to a quota of tens of thousands of trousers and shirts. In part, the reluctance of the EC to be more generous with Vietnam seems to reflect an unwillingness to part company radically with the United States. The risk is that if Vietnam does become another 'Asian tiger', Europe might once again lose out to an important market of 67 million people.

Australia

Despite its strong support for the United States during the Vietnam war (more than 6,000 Australian troops fought alongside the Americans), Australia has succeeded in recent years in forging stronger ties with Vietnam than probably any other western country. Following the election of a Labor government under Prime Minister Bob Hawke in 1983, Australia sought to adopt a more independent position than other western countries on the Cambodian conflict, offering to mediate between ASEAN and Vietnam on the issue. But a visit to Canberra by Vietnamese Foreign Minister Nguyen Co Thach in March 1984 failed to result in any new initiative.

Following, however, the failure of the 1989 Paris conference on Cambodia, the Australian government took the lead in sponsoring a study of the feasibility of a major UN involvement in Cambodia.[46] That study, which involved many visits to the region by the Australian Foreign Minister, Gareth Evans, led in 1990 to the adoption by the Security Council of the framework settlement for Cambodia. Since the promulgation of Vietnam's foreign investment code in 1988, Australia has become one of the five major foreign investors and, by the end of 1991, had more than $300 million invested, primarily in telecommunications, mining and tourism. In October 1991 it announced that it was resuming foreign aid to Vietnam, suspended since 1979.[47]

The United States and Japan

Despite the great improvement in its relations with China, ASEAN, the European Community and Australia, Vietnam continues to be shunned by the two most powerful economies in the world, the United States and Japan. It might seem unusual to treat these two in one breath, but it is striking that of all the advanced industrial countries Japan is now alone in following the American economic embargo against Vietnam. The United States has no diplomatic relations with Vietnam and, under the Trading with the Enemy Act, US companies are forbidden not only from investing, but also from trading with Vietnam. Although Japan has maintained diplomatic relations with Vietnam and has now replaced the Soviet Union as the country's largest trading partner, most of its private sector continues to observe an informal embargo of Vietnam. And – critically for the success of *doi moi* – Japan continues to support American efforts to block urgently needed international credits from the World Bank, the IMF and the Asian Development Bank.

There is little doubt that Japan would abandon its informal embargo the moment the United States does, and indeed there are signs that the Japanese government is already considering the resumption of limited aid to Vietnam. Normalization of relations with the United States remains therefore the most outstanding problem for Vietnamese foreign policy.

While the thrust of American policy has been to isolate Vietnam, the United States increasingly finds itself isolated over that policy. As noted, in the aftermath of the Paris conference on Cambodia in October 1991, the European Community, ASEAN and Australia moved swiftly to normalize relations. Yet Japan, despite maintaining its embargo, has already emerged in 1991 as Vietnam's largest trading partner. Until now, Tokyo has been faithfully following the United States as far as official bilateral aid is concerned. Among other things, this has resulted in disproportionately low Japanese investment in Vietnam. As of September 1991, Japan's roughly $100 million investment meant that it came only ninth on the list of foreign investors. However, Japanese companies have been preparing the groundwork for a major thrust into Vietnam as and when Tokyo resumes official development assistance. All the most important Japanese trading houses now have representative offices in Vietnam, and of the six foreign proposals currently being considered to invest in a major new oil refinery project, estimated to cost between $1 billion and $1.2 billion, four are from Japanese firms. A Japanese/ Vietnamese trade association in Hanoi already boasts 70 member companies. Since the signing of the Cambodian peace accord, Japanese business missions have been descending on Vietnam in record numbers, including a delegation from the influential federation of economic organizations, the Keidanren.[48]

Speculation of a shift in Japanese policy increased in early 1992, when the government initiated negotiations with Vietnam on the resumption of overseas development assistance (ODA). A delegation visited Vietnam in late January and appeared to have reached agreement on the repayment of an outstanding debt of $100 million from the old South Vietnamese government. With that problem solved, the conditions for a resumption of aid appear to be set. It is now expected that this will happen in the second half of 1992. As a possible sweetener for this eventuality, Vietnam will allow a Japanese company to explore for oil in the Gulf of Tonkin. Although the Japanese Foreign Minister is reported to have assured US Secretary of State James Baker in November 1991 that Japan would 'not make a big rush' in lifting its aid ban, the resumption of ODA is likely to lead to a significant increase in Japanese investment in Vietnam.[49]

Stripped of the conditions that various administrations have placed on normalization of relations with Vietnam, there remains the undeniable fact that Vietnam still touches a raw nerve in the United States. If one remembers that it was 1933 before the United States recognized the Soviet Union, and 1979 before it opened full diplomatic relations with the People's Republic of China, and given the humiliating circumstances in which the final US withdrawal took place, the sixteen years that have elapsed without diplomatic relations between the United States and Vietnam is less surprising. Resentment over that defeat, anguish over the deaths of 47,000 American servicemen and the failure to solve the question of those missing in action (MIAs) have haunted US policy towards Vietnam ever since. Indeed, it is remarkable that the Carter administration came close in 1978 to opening diplomatic relations with Vietnam, an initiative that came to grief because of Hanoi's demands for what amounted to war reparations and US fears of Chinese objections to any such move. Faced with a choice between the enormous benefits that were seen to accrue from a close relationship with China and the modest benefits that normalization with Vietnam would bring, President Carter opted for the former.[50]

With Vietnam's military intervention in Cambodia in December 1978, any prospect of a new relationship with Hanoi was precluded for successive administrations in Washington. Moreover, the conflict that ensued in Cambodia was seen in Washington against the larger mosaic of the global balance of power and the new cold war. Cambodia, together with Afghanistan, Angola and Nicaragua, were seen in Washington as evidence of a new Soviet assertiveness in the world. With the eclipse of normalization prospects, US administrations dealt with Vietnam through the filter of relations with ASEAN and, above all, China. For years after 1979 there seemed an absence of coherent policy on Indochina in Washington, and many observers concluded that the United States was content to sit back and allow the Soviet Union and China to dominate the fate of the peoples of Indochina. So much so that some worried that 'the United States may have gotten the worst of both worlds – a gradual political commitment to an involvement without being able to shape its eventual dimensions'.[51]

Throughout the 1980s the United States seemed constrained from making any new initiatives with regard to Vietnam by what it saw as its overall interests in East Asia, which dictated close ties with China. This picture remained substantially unchanged until the Tiananmen massacre and the failure of the 1989 Paris peace conference forced the United States to take a more active part in the search for peace in Cambodia. Yet the United States has always had other bilateral problems in its relationship with Vietnam, notably humanitarian issues. Indeed, successive administrations have laid equal weight on a resolution of the Cambodia conflict, and of the question of unaccounted MIAs, as the necessary preconditions for normalization of relations. Since August 1987, when General Vessey, the special presidential envoy on the MIA question, visited Vietnam for the first time, the United States has had an increasing degree of cooperation from Hanoi on this issue.[52] Beginning in September 1988, the two sides began conducting joint searches for the remains of MIAs. At the same time, the Vietnamese stepped up the orderly departure of Amerasian children and officers and officials of the former South Vietnamese government.

Prospects of a real breakthrough in relations between the two countries seemed encouraging in July 1990, when Secretary of State James Baker announced that the United States was willing to begin a dialogue with Vietnam on Cambodia.[53] Talks opened at the UN in New York in August, and at the end of September Mr Baker himself met in New York with Foreign Minister Nguyen Co Thach, the first meeting between the two countries' foreign ministers since the Paris peace conference of 1973.[54] Mr Thach later went to Washington for a meeting with General Vessey and Congressional leaders. In December the Assistant Secretary of State for East Asia, Richard Solomon, announced that the United States was ready to launch formal talks with Vietnam on normalizing relations. For a moment it seemed as if the Bush administration were moving to close the chapter on the Vietnam war.

But these early expectations were not met. The continuing unwillingness – well into 1991 – of Vietnam and its ally, the Phnom Penh government, to agree fully to the UN peace plan seems to have reawakened American fears of past Vietnamese diplomatic practice. Increasingly, the administration believed that Vietnam had to be kept to a rigid framework for normalization, which would force it to comply with the Cambodia settlement and the resolution of the MIA issue. As already noted, this framework, or 'roadmap', was presented to Trinh Xuan Long, the Vietnamese ambassador at the UN, by Richard Solomon in April 1991.[55] The roadmap defers the full establishment of diplomatic relations until after the holding of elections in Cambodia, an eventuality now not expected until March 1993. Ironically, two months after the presentation of the roadmap, the Phnom Penh government signified its willingness to accept the UN peace plan. If it had done so six months earlier, the straitjacket that the roadmap implies might not have been imposed.

Vietnam was disappointed by the delay in normalization that the roadmap indicates and by the continued linkage between that process and a settlement of the Cambodian conflict. Nevertheless, it did agree in late April 1991, following another visit to Hanoi by General Vessey, to the establishment of a US office in the Vietnamese capital to handle the MIA question. The United States also announced subsequently that it was giving a million dollars in humanitarian aid to Vietnam, the first such governmental aid since 1975. In July the two countries held another round of talks in Bangkok, while a further round took place at the UN in New York in November. The latter meeting led to the establishment of a working group on normalizing relations.[56] In March 1992, relations took a further modest step forward when Richard Solomon visited Hanoi, the most senior American official to do so since 1986. In exchange for enhanced cooperation on the MIA issue, Mr Solomon announced that the United States would give Vietnam $3 million in humanitarian aid. He reiterated, however, that there would be no deviation from the roadmap.[57]

What amounts to the isolation and punishment of Vietnam has continued to the present day, despite the acceptance by Hanoi of the UN peace agreement on Cambodia and the cooperation it has offered on the MIA issue. The United States has shown little inclination to deviate from the roadmap, even though it has been overtaken in many ways by subsequent events. Although the Bush administration frequently stated that its Middle East policy could not be dictated by the American hostages in Lebanon, it continues to allow its Vietnam policy to be dictated by the remains of American servicemen killed more than twenty years ago.

At the annual meeting in Bangkok of the World Bank and the IMF in October 1991, the United States blocked a French move that would have led to Vietnam being able to borrow once again from the international financial institutions.[58] The Treasury Department in Washington has also clamped down on dollar transactions between foreign banks and Vietnam. Further, the United States has continued to oppose the agreement between the United Kingdom and Vietnam for the repatriation of boat-people from Hong Kong, although less forcefully than in the past.[59] Remarks by Secretary Baker in Paris in October, and by President Bush in Singapore in January 1992, still link normalization to the Cambodia peace process and a full accounting for the MIAs, something that the United States has never demanded after any other war in which it was involved. Despite the public urging of such allies as Thailand, Australia and the United Kingdom, there now seems little likelihood of anything other than a modest improvement in relations between Washington and

Hanoi in 1992, an election year in the United States. Washington's unwillingness to respond seems to reflect an unresolved debate between the State Department, which with reservations wishes to normalize relations, and the White House, which at this stage in history sees no reason to help a communist regime that was also a former military enemy. The trauma of America's only defeat in war in two centuries still runs very deep and nowhere more so, it seems, than in the ranks of the Bush administration itself.[60]

6
CONCLUSION

'There are interpretations in some places that our party is intact, but has no future, that our party is no longer in its springtime, but only has old trees without any green sprouts. These worries are not unfounded.' *Nhan Dan*, cited in Reuters report, Hanoi, 14 January 1992.

Does communism have a future in Vietnam? The short answer to that question must be no, if one means by communism the classical Leninist doctrines and central planning. Even before the collapse of communist regimes in Eastern Europe, Vietnam had made a decisive shift towards a market economy, discarding the vestiges of central planning. In the past two years, as we have seen earlier, that process has gone even further, making a return to the old days of the plan seemingly impossible. Even party leaders no longer appear able to distinguish between communism and capitalism, at least in the economic realm, as Prime Minister Vo Van Kiet freely admitted in a recent BBC interview:

The contradiction may be in the ideology, in the forms of political institutions. But in the laws of development of each country, like the laws of economic development, particularly at this time, it's difficult to distinguish them, to say if this is capitalist and that is socialist.[1]

A more difficult question to pose is, Does the Communist Party of Vietnam have a future? Or, in other words, Can it continue to govern Vietnam and hold a monopoly of political power?

There can be little doubt that the Vietnamese Communist Party has been severely shaken by events in Eastern Europe, and even more so by those in the Soviet Union in 1991. As a veteran member of its Central Committee noted in an interview in Hanoi in November 1991, 'If the CPSU, which had been in power 74 years, can fall to pieces in 72 hours, we have at least to raise that possibility in Vietnam.'[2] Despite the continued brave face that the party itself puts on the future of socialism, or rather of communist party rule, such self-questioning is now widespread in Vietnam. Even from within party ranks there have been notable defectors from orthodoxy over the past three years, such as Tran Xuan Bach, Bui Tin and Nguyen Khac Vien. Most younger leaders must realize now that their careers will evolve in a non-communist world.

The accepted wisdom in the West appears to be that the rot in communism will be confined to Eastern Europe, that Asia is after all Asia, that the differences between the two are so great that the events of 1989 are unlikely to be repeated in Vietnam, China or North Korea (or, for that matter, Cuba).[3] The differences between Vietnamese communism and East European or Soviet communism are indeed very marked, and it is important to look at some of these for the bearing they may have on Vietnam's political and economic future. Perhaps most striking is that the revolution in Vietnam, like those in China and Cuba, had deep indigenous roots, and that the Communist Party has dominated the nationalist movement from before the Second World War and retains a great deal of popular support. Certainly, the Soviet Union had been generous with economic assistance and arms supplies during the war against the Americans in the 1960s, but this was in no way comparable with the direct imposition of communism *from above* by the Red Army in Eastern Europe in 1945. Thus, when the Soviet military guarantee of socialism in Eastern Europe was withdrawn by President Gorbachev after 1985, the very basis of communist rule was undermined.[4] It is worth noting, however, that even communist regimes long outside the Soviet orbit, such as Romania, Albania and Yugoslavia, were not immune to the seismic shock of the downfall of communism elsewhere.

Moreover, unlike their erstwhile comrades in Eastern Europe – even those in Hungary and Poland – the Vietnamese have proved far more adept and willing to embrace economic reform. In this endeavour they have made notable progress, leading to an albeit modest improvement in living standards for most Vietnamese. At the same time, while political reform has been limited in Vietnam, there has been an effective destalinization of everyday life since 1986, which can be readily seen in

Conclusion

easier contact with foreigners, greater access to information, and the abandonment of strict party control of the media, culture and entertainment.[5] Furthermore, for Vietnam, as for China, it is easier to join in the economic success of East Asia than it is for the East European countries to catch up with western Europe. The UN-brokered Cambodian peace settlement and Vietnam's rapidly improving relations with ASEAN, China and the EC have also considerably improved its economic chances. Historically, Vietnam has been much more open to the West than has China. And, stemming from this, at least in part, comes its greater capacity to respond to ideas and propositions originating in the outside world.

In other ways, too, Vietnam is distinct from the surviving communist regimes. Its system of collective leadership has survived intact through the decades of war, avoiding the personality-based regimes of North Korea and Cuba. And, while it now has many similarities with China, the Vietnamese party has not turned in on itself or turned the army on the people, as the Chinese party has done. Indeed, although not without its blemishes, such as the land reform campaign of 1956 or the 're-education' programme in South Vietnam after 1975, Vietnam's human rights record is probably considerably better than China's. The widespread purges and terror tactics that marred Soviet and Chinese party history have been avoided. Vietnam's Communist Party is still committed, too, to a measure of political reform.

Although many of these characteristics point to Vietnamese communism having a longer shelf-life than many of its counterparts, there are also countervailing tendencies undermining party rule. In the first place, although communism has been in power in the North for almost four decades, the party has ruled in the southern half only since 1975. And, as already noted, there was little mass support for liberation in 1975, especially in the cities. The memory of the pre-communist era is still strong in the South, and a visitor to Ho Chi Minh City today might well conclude that the old Saigon was reasserting itself. What is undoubtedly clear is that the old North/South divide is now greater than ever, ironically in large part because of the success of the economic reforms. Not surprisingly, the South is far more in tune with *doi moi* than the North. Some 60% of all foreign investment in Vietnam is concentrated in Ho Chi Minh City, and 80% in southern Vietnam generally. Saigonese regard it as an accident of history that they are ruled from Hanoi. The country's much-vaunted turnaround from being a net rice importer to being the world's number three rice exporter is largely due to the peasant farmers of the Mekong delta.[6] More than 90% of the rice exports in the best year so far, 1989, came from this region. At the same time many of the social problems associated with development, particularly unemployment, are most marked in the South.

While throughout Vietnam there is a growing independence from the Communist Party and a burgeoning 'civil society', the process is most marked in southern Vietnam. One symptom of this is a renewal of support for traditional southern religious sects, such as the Cao Dai movement, a revival in fortune-telling and the restoration of Buddhist temples.[7] Another sign was the emergence of the dissident Club of Former Resistance Fighters in the South in recent years. Southern cultural life is also increasingly distinct from that of the North. And in the South, more than in the North, there is widespread disenchantment among the population at large with the sacrifices made in the anti-US war and in Cambodia. These differences between the two halves of the country would pose a problem for any government, but the danger for Hanoi is that the growing differentiation will assume an anti-communist character.

Of the remaining communist regimes, with the possible exception of Cuba, Vietnam has been the most affected by the collapse of communism in Eastern Europe and the Soviet Union. Through its membership of Comecon and its 1978 treaty of friendship with the Soviet Union, Vietnam was closely tied to Eastern Europe. More than 300,000 Vietnamese workers were resident there in 1989, and tens of thousands of specialists and students have been trained in the former communist countries. The economic consequences of the fall of those regimes have already been dealt with in this study; the ideological consequences have similarly been great. The Vietnamese Communist Party had seen its struggle for national liberation as one front in a worldwide battle for socialism. The demise of communism as an international ideology has therefore weakened the legitimacy of party rule in Vietnam itself. This has suffered a further blow by the effective separation of the political destinies of Laos and Cambodia from that of Vietnam. After sixty years of struggle, the Vietnamese Communist Party has been forced to confront the fact that Indochina is no longer a single strategic terrain. Vietnam has also had to reconcile itself to the uncomfortable fact that rule by an allied party in Cambodia will give way to UN-supervised elections, an event which is bound to have an effect on southern Vietnam.

It is difficult to avoid the conclusion that the collapse of communism in the Soviet Union, the motherland of revolution, has been a devastating political and psychological blow to the leadership in Hanoi. There has been a notable defensiveness in official party statements and evidence that a real soul-searching is in progress. Even before the August coup in Moscow, the outgoing party leader, Nguyen Van Linh, noted at the seventh party congress:

> The overall and profound crisis in the socialist countries has caused socialism to be subjected to unprecedented and severe criticism from many directions. It is regrettable that even from the ranks of communists there have been manifestations of indecision in terms of political stance, and trends negating the achievement of socialism, leading to the negating of the socialist path altogether.[8]

In January 1992 the Politburo member Vu Oanh delivered a blistering attack in the party newspaper, *Nhan Dan*, against widespread corruption and inefficiency, and called for a drive to regain popular support if the party is to survive. The same day the newspaper reported falling party membership in many areas of the country. Citing the province of Hai Hung, near Hanoi, it reported that annual recruits, who had numbered 2,000 in the years 1979–88, had fallen to 1,718 in 1989, 1,237 in 1990 and to barely 500 in the first six months of 1991. Some districts had not recruited a single new member in years. One district reported 200 members quitting in 1990, some of whom had 'occupied high places at the provincial level and others had been party members for 40 years'.[9] There is reason to believe that this pattern is repeating itself nationwide.

The reform programme that the party initiated in 1986 and has pursued ever since is itself a tacit admission that socialist economics did not work and that the communist social transformation was a disaster. The party's right to rule by virtue of its being the proletarian vanguard is being undermined by the stress now on economic competence and efficiency. As younger leaders take over from the founding generation, other causes besides simply maintaining party power will come to seem more important in the national interest. The removal of party controls over the peasantry, through the abandonment of collectivization, and over urban residents, through the encouragement of private enterprise, is also weakening party control and morale. The party has moved from being the orthodox implementer of the plan, to being the dominant political force in a market economy.

The Vietnamese Communist Party, if it is to survive, may end up being not that different from the Kuomintang in Taiwan, the People's

Action Party in Singapore or Golkar in Indonesia, models which many Vietnamese talk favourably of in private now. Some of the political reforms currently under discussion, such as divorcing the party from the government, would appear to encourage this trend. But if the party is going to move in this direction, it still has a lot to divest itself of from its past. But just as Vietnam's leadership already sees its economic future converging with that of ASEAN, so its political future may increasingly lie in that direction as well.

NOTES

Chapter 1: Introduction

1 Humphrey Hawksley, 'Hanoi's relations with Moscow near watershed', *The Times*, 15 March 1989.

2 See W. Brus and K. Lushin's aptly titled *From Marx to the Market*, Cambridge University Press, 1989; and Philip Hanson, 'Is there a "Third Way" between Capitalism and Socialism?', *Reports on the USSR*, RFE/RL Research Institute, 30 August 1991, vol. 3, no. 35, pp. 15–19, especially page 18: 'It also remains to be seen whether it is possible, having made the institutional changes, to get the desired results in terms of prosperity sufficiently quickly. But experience in both the East and the West supports the conclusion that, the more quickly the jump across this no-man's land can be made, the better.' See also Judy Batt, *East Central Europe from Reform to Transformation*, Royal Institute of International Affairs and Pinter, London, 1991. On the link between authoritarianism and economic development in Asia, see 'Freedom and Prosperity', *The Economist*, 29 June 1991, pp. 17–21, especially the interview with Lee Kuan Yew.

Chapter 2: The historical background

1 John T. McAlister, Jr., and Paul Mus, *The Vietnamese and Their Revolution*, Harper and Row, New York and London, 1970, p. 34.

2 David Marr, *Vietnamese Anticolonialism*, University of California, Berkeley and London, 1971, p. 20.

3 Ibid., p. 11; Truong Buu Lam, *Patterns of Vietnamese Response to Foreign Intervention*, Yale University Monograph Series, New Haven, 1967, pp. 49–54; and Nguyen Khac Vien, *Vietnam: A Long History*, Foreign Languages Publishing House, Hanoi, 1987, pp. 32–143.

4 Huynh Kim Khanh, *Vietnamese Communism 1925–1945*, Cornell Univer-

sity Press, Ithaca and London, 1982, p. 32.

5 Marr, *Vietnamese Anticolonialism*, pp. 30–53, 185–8; Vien, *Vietnam*, pp. 147–65.

6 Marr, *Vietnamese Anticolonialism*, pp. 185ff.

7 Ibid., p. 203; see also Jean Chesneaux, *Contribution à l'Histoire de la Nation Vietnamienne*, Editions Sociales, Paris, 1955, pp. 183–205.

8 McAlister and Mus, *The Vietnamese and Their Revolution*, p. 36.

9 See, in particular, James C. Scott, *The Moral Economy of the Peasant: Rebellion and Subsistence in Southeast Asia*, Yale University Press, New Haven, 1976, and Samuel L. Popkin, *The Rational Peasant: The Political Economy of Rural Society in Vietnam*, University of California Press, Berkeley and London, 1979.

10 In the first month of the battle alone, 16,000 of the Viet Minh were killed. See Giap's comments, cited by Jonathan Mirsky, 'Reconsidering Vietnam', *The New York Review of Books*, 10 October 1991, p. 46.

11 Jean Lacoutoure, *Vietnam: Between the Truces*, Secker and Warburg, London, 1966, p. 10; Carlyle A. Thayer, *War by Other Means: National Liberation and Revolution in Vietnam*, Allen & Unwin, Sydney, 1989, pp. 3–6.

12 Khanh, *Vietnamese Communism*, p. 40, fn. 11.

13 The literature on the American war in the South is immense, but see, in particular, Neil Sheehan, *A Bright Shining Lie: John Paul Vann and America in Vietnam*, Picador, London, 1990; Stanley Karnow, *Vietnam: A History*, Viking, New York, 1983; George McT. Kahin, *Intervention: How America Became Involved in Vietnam*, Alfred A. Knopf, New York, 1986; and Frances Fitzgerald, *Fire in the Lake: The Vietnamese and the Americans in Vietnam*, Vintage Books, New York, 1972.

14 See Eric M. Bergerud, *The Dynamics of Defeat: The Vietnam War in Hau Nghia Province*, Westview Press, Boulder, San Francisco and Oxford, 1991; Jeffrey Race, *War Comes to Long An*, University of California Press, Berkeley, 1972.

15 Van Tien Dung, *Our Great Spring Victory: An Account of the Liberation of South Vietnam*, Monthly Review Press, New York, 1977.

16 See, *inter alia*, Bergerud, *Dynamics of Defeat*, and Mirsky, 'Reconsidering Vietnam'.

17 Sheehan, *Bright Shining Lie*.

Chapter 3: The political background

1 See Huynh Kim Khanh, *Vietnamese Communism 1925–1945*, Cornell University Press, Ithaca and London, 1982, p. 36, fn. 2.

2 See, for example, the commentary by Phuc Cuong, '35 Years of Struggle on the International Front', *Tap Chi Cong San* (Communist Review),

reprinted in *Vietnam Courier*, vol. 16, no. 9, September 1980, pp. 6–9, especially p. 8: 'the dauntless struggle of the Vietnamese people against US imperialism had major significance in the context of the destiny of the world and the world revolutionary movement ... It is in this sense that the victory of the Vietnamese people and the defeat of US imperialism have made significant contributions to changing the world balance of forces and averting the danger of another world war.' See also *Vietnam Courier*, vol. 16, no. 3, March 1980, p. 1, which goes so far as to claim, 'History has entrusted the Vietnamese people with heavy responsibilities and required them to be in the front line of peoples fighting for the noble objectives of all humanity'.

3 On the background, see Khanh, *Vietnamese Communism*, pp. 35–126.

4 For a consideration of Ho Chi Minh's life see Daniel Hemery, *Ho Chi Minh: de l'Indochine au Vietnam*, Gallimard, Paris, 1990. On Ho's early years see David Marr's stimulating *Vietnamese Anticolonialism*, University of California, Berkeley and London, 1971, pp. 253–60, and Khanh, *Vietnamese Communism*, pp. 57–66.

5 William J. Duiker, *The Communist Road to Power in Vietnam*, Westview Press, Boulder, Colorado, 1981, p. 13.

6 See Khanh, *Vietnamese Communism*, p. 187.

7 Ibid., p. 340.

8 For an eyewitness account, see Tiziano Terzani, *Giai Phong! The Fall and Liberation of Saigon*, St Martin's Press, New York, 1976, p. 88.

9 Duiker, *Road to Power*, p. 269; see also Douglas Pike, *War, Peace and the Viet Cong*, M.I.T. Press, Cambridge, MA, 1969, p. 128. He estimates 75,000 dead by the end of August 1968.

10 On re-education see *Report of an Amnesty International Mission to the Socialist Republic of Vietnam, 1979*, Amnesty International Publications, London, 1981. This writer was a member of the delegation and author of the report. On a visit to Ho Chi Minh City in November 1991 two prominent former communists described re-education as the single biggest mistake the party made in the South in the aftermath of the war.

11 It is interesting to note, however, that in September 1975 the Provisional Revolutionary Government of South Vietnam did apply for separate membership of the United Nations. In another characteristically short-sighted move by the United States the application was vetoed. See Carlyle Thayer, 'Political Development in Vietnam 1975–85', in Colin Mackeras, Robert Cribb and Allan Healy, *Contemporary Vietnam: Perspectives from Australia*, University of Wollongong Press, Wollongong, 1987, p. 65.

12 On political developments after 1975, see William J. Duiker, *Vietnam Since the Fall of Saigon*, Ohio University Press, Athens, Ohio, 1990, pp. 3–119; and Thayer, 'Political Development'. For a flavour of official

attitudes at the time, see *Vietnam: Vers une Nouvelle Étape*, Foreign Languages Press, Hanoi, 1977.

13 William Turley, 'Vietnam Since Reunification', *Problems of Communism*, vol. XXVI, no. 1, March–April 1977, p. 44.

14 Carlyle Thayer, 'Political Developments in Vietnam: From the 6th to 7th National Party Congress', October 1991, p. 2.

15 After his death, however, Ho's wishes not to be revered have been ignored by his erstwhile comrades who, against his express wishes to be cremated, built a mausoleum for his mummified corpse in Hanoi. See Hemery, *Ho Chi Minh*, pp. 163–5; and, on the latterday cult of Ho, see Terry McCarthy, 'Vietnam seeks salvation from its dead hero', *Independent*, 4 August 1990.

16 On the defection of Hoang Van Hoan see Nayan Chanda, *Brother Enemy: The War after the War*, Collier Books, New York, 1986, pp. 379–80.

17 On Linh's removal in 1982 from the Politburo see Michael Williams, 'The Fifth Congress of the Vietnamese Communist Party', *Communist Affairs*, vol. 1, no. 4, October 1982, pp. 783–7. Linh had long been a strong advocate of economic reforms and had played an active role in promoting them when he was party secretary in Ho Chi Minh City from 1981 to 1986.

18 On the sixth party congress see Thayer, 'Political Development', 1991; Michael C. Williams, 'The Sixth Congress of the Vietnamese Communist Party', *Journal of Communist Studies*, vol. 3, no. 2, June 1987, pp. 185–90; my 'Vietnam: The Slow Road to Reform' in David S.G. Goodman, *Communism and Reform in East Asia*, Frank Cass, London, 1988, pp. 102–12; 'The Vietnam Party Congress and Aftermath', FBIS Analysis Report, FB 87–10005, 5 March 1987; and 'Vietnam: Prospects for Progress', Foreign and Commonwealth Office, London, April 1987.

19 Le Duc Tho, 'Pressing Tasks in Party-Building Work', *BBC Summary of World Broadcasts* (hereafter *SWB*), FE/8257/B7f, 13 May 1986.

20 On the freer atmosphere after 1986, see Carlyle A. Thayer, 'Political reform in Vietnam: Doi Moi and the emergence of civil society' in Robert F. Miller, *The Developments of Civil Society in Communist Systems*, Allen & Unwin, Sydney, 1992, pp. 110–29; see also John H. Esterline, 'Vietnam in 1987: Steps towards Rejuvenation', *Asian Survey*, January 1988, vol. XXVIII, no. 1, pp. 86–94; Barry Wain, 'Vietnam undergoes another revolution', *Asian Wall Street Journal*, 30 June 1988; and David Watts, 'Media campaign paves way for Vietnam reform', *The Times*, 20 November 1987. One Western journalist claims that most of the 'NVL' articles were in fact ghost written by Bui Tin, one of the senior editors of *Nhan Dan*, who later defected to the West. See Steve Vines, 'Vietnam tastes its own perestroika', *The Observer*, 17 April 1988.

21 See Murray Hiebert, 'Cadres Called to Account', *Far Eastern Economic*

Review (hereafter *FEER*), 11 June 1987, pp. 38, and his 'Renovation of Newspapers', *FEER*, 10 September 1987; Ronald J. Cimia, 'Vietnam in 1988: The Brink of Renewal', *Asian Survey*, January 1989, vol. XXIX, no. 1, pp. 64–72.

22 For more details see Thayer, 'Political Developments', p. 8.

23 See Wain, 'Vietnam undergoes another revolution'.

24 See Michael Williams, 'Vietnam', in *The Asia and Pacific Review*, World of Information, Saffron Walden, 1989, pp. 244–5.

25 Interviews with Huynh Son Phuoc, editor of *Tuoi Tre*, Vietnam's leading investigative newspaper, and Vu Tuat Viet, editor of *Saigon Giai Phong*, Ho Chi Minh City, 23 November 1991. See also Barbara Crossette, 'Vietnamese Press Tries its Hand at Some "Real Reporting"', *International Herald Tribune*, 9 September 1987. Despite some difficulties with the authorities it is above all these two papers, *Tuoi Tre* and *Saigon Giai Phong*, that have shown greatest independence from the Communist Party.

26 The renaissance of Vietnamese art and culture since 1986 is one of the most remarkable and enduring results of *doi moi*. See Barbara Crossette, 'In Vietnam, a Literary Renaissance', *International Herald Tribune*, 12 August 1987, and her 'In Vietnam, Quiet Anger', *Inter-national Herald Tribune*, 24 April 1988; Murray Hiebert, 'People's Art Comes Closer to the People', *FEER*, 10 September 1987, pp. 49–51, and his 'New Chapter Opens as Writers Reflect Reality', *FEER*, 8 September 1988, pp. 107–9; and Barry Wain, 'Pitiful Writer Jolts Vietnamese Minds', *Asian Wall Street Journal Weekly*, 13 August 1990.

27 See Thayer, 'Political Developments', pp. 5–6.

28 Interviews with Madame Ngo Ba Thanh, Chairperson of the National Assembly law commission, New York, 13 September 1991, and Hanoi, 16 November 1991. See also her *Legal and Political Reforms in Vietnam Today*, Law Commission of the National Assembly, Hanoi, 1991.

29 See *Vietnam: Renovation (doi moi), the Law and Human Rights in the 1990s*, Amnesty International, London, 1990.

30 Murray Hiebert, 'Reforming Pains', *FEER*, 17 March 1988.

31 Murray Hiebert, 'Cheer in Cholon', *FEER*, 4 August 1988. A more tolerant attitude towards religious groups and especially towards the Catholic Church was also evident after the sixth party congress. See David Watts, 'Hanoi and church attempt to bury mutual suspicions', *The Times*, 24 November 1987; Michael Fathers, 'Vietnam cautious as Catholic Church presses for acceptance', *Independent*, 23 August 1988; and David Brunnstrom, 'Vietnamese Catholicism enjoys renaissance despite restrictions', Reuters News Agency, Hanoi, 5 January 1992. About 10% of Vietnam's 67 million people are estimated to be Catholics. Unlike in China or North Korea, the Catholic Church has never been banned in Vietnam.

32 See Carlyle A. Thayer, 'Hanoi Moves More Cautiously on Reform', *International Herald Tribune*, 5 August 1988.

33 Barbara Crossette, 'Hanoi Jails Writers and a Journalist In an Apparent Warning on Dissent', *International Herald Tribune*, 6 July 1988.

34 Steven Erlanger, 'Vietnam's Perestroika Spurs a Debate', *International Herald Tribune*, 25 April 1989; Michael Williams, 'Vietnam', pp. 228–30.

35 Michael Williams, 'Vietnam's New Hard Line – The Seventh Central Committee Plenum', *Journal of Communist Studies*, vol. 6, no. 1, March 1990, pp. 112–13; Michael Richardson, 'Hard-Line Vietnam Chides Poland and Hungary', *International Herald Tribune*, 7 September 1989. For Vietnamese handling of the events of June 1989 in China, see Carlyle Thayer, 'China's Domestic Crisis and Vietnamese Responses, April–July 1989' in Gary Klintworth, ed., *China's Crisis: The International Implications*, Canberra Papers on Strategy and Defence no. 57, Australian National University, 1989, pp. 83–97.

36 Nicholas Cumming-Bruce, 'Vietnam's old warriors try to freeze political debate', *Guardian*, 18 December 1989, and his 'Vietnam holds firm against tide of reform', *Guardian*, 30 December 1989.

37 On the eighth plenum, see Michael Williams, 'The Soviet-Asian Connection', *FEER*, 17 May 1990; Nicholas Cumming-Bruce, 'Hanoi prepares for watershed plenum', *Guardian*, 29 January 1990, and his 'Vietnam puts brakes on party reform', *Guardian*, 27 April 1990; Roger Matthews, 'Vietnamese party wraps up against wind of change', *The Financial Times*, 30 March 1990; interview with Bui Tin, 5 March 1992, London.

38 See Thayer, 'Political Development', pp. 15–17; Nayan Chanda, 'Force for Change', *FEER*, 5 October 1989, pp. 24–5; and Barry Wain, 'Old Revolutionaries in Vietnam Launch One Last Offensive', *Asian Wall Street Journal*, 8 May 1989. In May 1990 several members of the Club of Former Resistance Fighters were placed under arrest by the authorities, who feared demonstrations in Ho Chi Minh City on the occasion of the centenary of Ho's birth. See Jean-Claude Pomonti, 'La direction du PC entend gérer elle-même le changement', *Le Monde*, 23 May 1990.

39 For the views of Bui Tin see his *Pétition d'un citoyen*, Paris, 1990, and his 'Une ouverture verrouillée', *Le Monde*, 22 June 1991; see also Jean-Claude Pomonti, 'Un responsable du quotidien du PC réclame l'élection démocratique d'une nouvelle Assemblée', *Le Monde*, 30 November 1990, and Thayer, 'Political Developments', p. 21. In a petition circulated in January 1991, the historian Dr Nguyen Khac Vien described the current Vietnamese leadership as 'totally impotent, plunging the country into disorder and preventing all development'. See 'M. Nguyen Khac Vien réclame la dissolution des organes dirigeants du PC', *Le Monde*, 5 March 1991, and Steven Erlanger, 'Vietnamese Historian Urges Greater Freedom', *International Herald Tribune*, 6 March 1991. On the

arrest of Duong Thu Huong, see 'Vives protestations en France après l'arrestation de Mme Duong Thu Huong', *Le Monde*, 15 May 1991. She was released in November following a visit to Vietnam by the French Foreign Minister, Roland Dumas. See *Le Monde*, 21 November 1991.

40 Interviews with officials and academics in Hanoi, November 1991.

41 See *Communist Party of Vietnam 7th National Congress: Documents*, Foreign Languages Press, Hanoi, 1991; see also Carlyle A. Thayer, 'Vietnam: The Party Gathers at the Fork in the Road', *International Herald Tribune*, 22–3 June 1991; Nayan Chanda, 'Hard-Liners Shape Role of Vietnam Reformers', *Asian Wall Street Journal Weekly*, 8 July 1991; Michael C. Williams, 'Vietnam: The Seventh Party Congress', *Journal of Communist Studies*, vol. 7, no. 4, December 1991, pp. 535–9; Jean-Claude Pomonti, 'Vietnam: le renouvellement de la direction après le VIIe congrès du PC', *Le Monde*, 28 June 1991.

42 Chanda, 'Hard-Liners'.

43 Thayer, 'Political Developments', p. 22.

44 See Jean-Claude Pomonti, 'Un entretien avec le premier ministre vietnamien', *Le Monde*, 15 October 1991. In this connection it is interesting to note that the Hanoi Polytechnic director, Ho Huu Trac – now deputy minister for education – is not a party member, but all other senior ministers are thought to be party members.

45 See 'Hanoi's Constitution Opens to Enterprise', *International Herald Tribune*, 31 December 1991; and Alexander Nicoll, 'Vietnam charts course for political reform', *The Financial Times*, 31 December 1991.

Chapter 4: Reform and the economy

1 On Vietnam's economic reforms, see Per Ronnas and Orjan Sjoberg, 'Economic Reform in Vietnam: Dismantling the Centrally Planned Economy', *Journal of Communist Studies*, forthcoming, 1992; Adam Fforde, *The Political Economy of Reform in Vietnam – Some Reflections*, paper given at Harvard Institute for International Development, 19 March 1991; *Indochina Country Profile 1991–92*, Economist Intelligence Unit, London, 1991, pp. 6–10, 13–16; and United Nations Development Programme (hereafter UNDP), *Report on the Economy of Vietnam*, State Planning Committee, Hanoi, 1990.

2 Fforde, *Political Economy*, p. 1.

3 'Strategy for Socioeconomic Stabilization and Development up to the Year 2000', *7th National Congress: Documents*, p. 179; see also Alexander Nicoll, 'Striding to the market', *The Financial Times*, 13 November 1991.

4 See Fforde, *Political Economy*, p. 21: 'the Vietnamese economy today is one where the majority of inputs and outputs are bought and sold voluntarily by independent units who base their decisions primarily upon consid-

erations of profit, price and personal welfare'.

5 William J. Duiker, *Vietnam Since the Fall of Saigon*, Ohio University Monographs in International Studies, Athens, Ohio, 1989, pp. 3–39; and William S. Turley, 'Vietnam Since Reunification', *Problems of Communism*, vol. XXVI, no. 2, March–April 1977, pp. 36–54.

6 Fforde, *Political Economy*, pp. 5–6; and interviews with economists in Hanoi, November 1991.

7 'Vietnam's Economy in 1983: Impact of New Economic Policies', *Vietnam Courier*, no. 2, 1984, pp. 12–13.

8 T. Kimura, *The Vietnamese Economy*, Institute of Developing Economies, Tokyo, 1989, p. 31.

9 'Ho Chi Minh City and the Economic Development of the Region', *Vietnam Courier*, no. 1, 1984, pp. 10–13.

10 Gareth Porter, 'The Politics of "Renovation" in Vietnam', *Problems of Communism*, vol. 39, no. 3, May–June 1990, pp. 72–88.

11 'An Economic Reform with a Revolutionary Character', *Vietnam Courier*, no. 10, 1985, pp. 10–12.

12 Porter, 'Politics of Renovation', p. 77.

13 *BBC Summary of World Broadcasts* (hereafter *SWB*), 17 December 1986, FE/8444/C1/6.

14 Douglas Pike, *Vietnam and the Soviet Union*, Westview Press, Boulder, Colorado, 1987, pp. 138–40; Carlyle A. Thayer and Ramesh Thakur, *Soviet Relations with India and Vietnam*, Macmillan, London, 1991, pp. 186–97.

15 Murray Hiebert, 'Converting to Trade', *Far Eastern Economic Review* (hereafter *FEER*), 27 April 1989, pp. 72–3.

16 BBC *SWB*, 16 December 1986, FE/8443/C2/2.

17 V. Mikheyev, 'Privatization in Newly Industrialized Countries: Useful Lessons', *Far Eastern Affairs*, no. 1, 1990, pp. 52–67.

18 There was some recognition of this important point at the sixth congress. In his Economic Report, Vo Van Kiet stressed that the renovation process involved an element of new thinking and intellectual freedom. He urged the party to implement incentive policies to create favourable conditions for those considered a 'valuable asset' to the country's development. See BBC *SWB*, 23 December 1986, FE/8449/C1/9.

19 Kimura, *Vietnamese Economy*, p. 64; see also Barry Wain, 'Vietnam's Plight Worsens As Food Supplies Dwindle', *Wall Street Journal*, 11 May 1988.

20 UNDP, *Economy of Vietnam*, pp. 17–18; and Duiker, *Vietnam*, pp. 247–8. The name of the Peasants' Association was changed by dropping the word 'collective' from the title so that private farmers could join. I am grateful to Carl Thayer for this information.

21 Keith Richburg, 'Vietnam Tastes the Profit Motive', *International Herald*

Tribune, 16 July 1987; Michael Fathers, 'Ho Chi Minh City takes capitalist road to prosperity', *Independent*, 16 September 1988; see also R.J. Cima, 'Vietnam's Economic Reform: Approaching the 1990s', *Asian Survey*, vol. XXIX, no. 8, August 1989, pp. 786–99.

22 'Vietnam Drafts Foreign Venture Law', *International Herald Tribune*, 18 August 1987; Nick Cumming-Bruce, 'Vietnam law opens the doors to foreign currency investment', *Guardian*, 31 December 1987; Nguyen Xuan Oanh, 'A Vietnamese Assesses Hanoi's Attempt at Perestroika', *International Herald Tribune*, 13 December 1988; for the text see 'Vietnamese Law on Foreign Investment', BBC *SWB*, 13 January 1988, FE/0047.

23 Murray Hiebert, 'Looking Outward', *FEER*, 27 April 1989, p. 70.

24 See interview with Dr Nguyen Ngoc Ha, Deputy Head of the Central Board for Overseas Vietnamese, in *Vietnam Courier*, no. 5, 1990, p. 16.

25 BBC *SWB*, 3 April 1991, FE/W0173 A/10; Murray Hiebert, 'Wooing Them Home', *FEER*, 23 January 1992, pp. 18–19.

26 Murray Hiebert, 'The Tilling Fields', *FEER*, 10 May 1990, pp. 32–4.

27 John Elliott, 'Vietnam lures foreign explorers', *The Financial Times*, 15 March 1989; Barry Wain, 'Vietnam Offers West Selected Opportunities', *Wall Street Journal*, 12 July 1989; and Roger Matthews, 'Thais send trade mission to Vietnam', *The Financial Times*, 19 May 1989.

28 UNDP, *Economy of Vietnam*, pp. 18–19.

29 Murray Hiebert, 'Fiscal Interdiction', *FEER*, 29 March 1989, pp. 22–3.

30 Murray Hiebert, 'Going for a Dong', *FEER*, 19 September 1991, p. 68.

31 'About the Fight Against Inflation in Vietnam', *Vietnam Courier*, no. 3, 1990, p. 10; Economist Intelligence Unit, *Indochina: Vietnam, Laos, Cambodia*, no. 3, 1991, p. 20.

32 Economist Intelligence Unit, *Indochina*, p. 22.

33 Interviews with economists in Ho Chi Minh City, November 1991; 'Vietnam lays off 550,000 workers', Agence France Presse (hereafter AFP), Hanoi, 28 May 1991; 'Vietnam's jobless pin hopes on private enterprise', AFP, 6 August 1991.

34 *The Financial Times*, 15 August 1990.

35 'Vietnam smuggling hurts local industry', Reuters News Agency, Hanoi, 30 August 1991.

36 'Vietnam newspaper reports surge in big money frauds', Reuters, Hanoi, 9 September 1991; 'Vietnam corruption', Reuters, Hanoi, 4 October 1991.

37 *Nhan Dan*, 31 January 1992, reported by AFP, Hanoi, 31 January 1992.

38 On difficulties faced by investors see Murray Hiebert, 'The Rise of Saigon', *FEER*, 5 September 1991; and Stefan Wagstyl, 'Still the domain of the trader', *The Financial Times*, 14 November 1991.

39 'British-Vietnam co-operation in oil exploration', *Vietnam Courier*, no. 4, 1989, p. 3.

40 Steven Erlanger, 'Vietnam's Gains Slip Away', *International Herald Tribune*, 19 February 1991.

41 'Vietnam to ease investment code soon, premier says', AFP, Hanoi, 31 January 1992; interview with Dr Nguyen Mai, Deputy Chairman of the State Committee for Cooperation and Investment, Hanoi, November 1991.

42 Murray Hiebert, 'Crisis Management', *FEER*, 19 December 1991, p. 22; Alexander Nicoll, 'Striding to the market', *The Financial Times*, 13 November 1991.

43 Interviews in Hanoi, November 1991.

44 Interviews with UNDP officials, see also UNDP, *Economy of Vietnam*.

Chapter 5: The foreign policy context

1 Murray Hiebert, 'Steps to a Summit', *Far Eastern Economic Review* (hereafter *FEER*), 3 October 1991; Murray Hiebert and Michael Vatikiotis, 'ASEAN's Embrace', *FEER*, 14 November 1991.

2 Interview with Dr Richard Rigby, Director of Indochina Division, Australian Ministry of Foreign Affairs, Hanoi, 14 November 1991.

3 Interviews with officials in Hanoi; see also Michael Leifer and John Phipps, *Vietnam and Doi Moi: Domestic and International Dimensions of Reform*, Discussion Paper no. 35, Royal Institute of International Affairs, London, 1991, pp. 30–31.

4 See Kay Magistad, 'Japanese Poised for Rush Into Vietnam', *International Herald Tribune*, 3 January 1991.

5 Leifer and Phipps, *Vietnam and Doi Moi*, p. 23.

6 Ibid.; see also Ma Zongshi, 'Perestroika In Vietnam: A Balance Sheet', *Indochina Report*, no. 17, October–December 1988.

7 Leifer and Phipps, *Vietnam and Doi Moi*, p. 27.

8 Interviews in Hanoi with Soviet diplomats, November 1991.

9 See Nayan Chanda's classic account *Brother Enemy*; and Robert S. Ross, *The Indochina Tangle: China's Vietnam Policy 1975–1979*, Columbia University Press, New York, 1988.

10 For the text see Daniel Hemery, *Ho Chi Minh: de l'Indochine au Vietnam*, Gallimard, Paris, 1990, pp. 163–5.

11 Lucian Pye has noted, 'the Hanoi government, which had an exaggerated idea of the amount of support it could expect from abroad, became surprisingly dependent on the Soviet Union. The intensity of Vietnamese nationalism in opposing French and, earlier, Chinese colonial domination led many observers to underestimate the Vietnamese craving for dependent ties with a properly nurturing authority.' Lucian W. Pye, *Asian Power and Politics: The Cultural Dimensions of Authority*, Harvard University Press, Cambridge, MA, 1985, p. 240.

12 Interview with Deng Xiaoping, *Time*, 12 March 1979.

13 The section on foreign policy in the political report, for example, speaks only of relations between Vietnam and the Soviet Union 'being renewed in accordance with the interests of each people'. *7th National Congress*, p. 89; the Political Programme is even vaguer and talks only of consolidating and developing 'the traditional relations of friendship and cooperation with other socialist countries'. Ibid., p. 61.

14 See Michael C. Williams, 'New Soviet Policy Toward Southeast Asia', *Asian Survey*, vol. XXXI, no. 4, April 1991, pp. 364–77.

15 The turning point in the relationship was probably marked by the first Sino-Soviet talks on Cambodia held in Peking in August 1988. Interview with Igor Rogachev, Soviet Deputy Foreign Minister for Asian Affairs, Moscow, March 1990; see also Nayan Chanda, 'A Troubled Friendship', *FEER*, 9 June 1988, and Jonathan Pollack, 'Moscow Takes a Hard Look at Ties with Vietnam', *FEER*, 22 September 1988.

16 Vietnam is still in debt to the former Soviet Union by a considerable amount, estimated at 10 billion roubles or $15 billion. Some economic links are likely to survive, such as Vietsovpetro, the only oil-producing joint venture so far, which earned $580 million in 1991. Agence France Presse (hereafter AFP), Hanoi, 2 January 1991. At the end of 1991 there was still a limited Soviet naval presence at Cam Ranh Bay, although this was much reduced compared with past years. A Soviet official in June 1991 was quoted as saying that the remaining Soviet forces would be withdrawn by 1994. See 'Aide Says Soviets Still Plan to Quit Base In Vietnam', *International Herald Tribune*, 19 June 1991; see also Sophie Quinn-Judge, 'Cam Ranh Mushrooms', *FEER*, 23 January 1992, p. 17.

17 See *Statement of the Five Permanent Members of the Security Council of the United Nations on Cambodia*, United Nations, New York, 28 August 1990.

18 See Leifer and Phipps, *Vietnam and Doi Moi*, p. 22; for the 1991 statement see 'Political Report of the Central Committee at the 7th National Congress' in *Communist Party of Vietnam 7th National Congress: Documents*, Foreign Languages Publishing House, Hanoi, 1991, p. 89. See pp. 90-91, at the end of the foreign relations section, for the rather cryptic comment, 'We have also, in a number of cases, failed to reach complete unanimity both in perception and action'.

19 'Political Programme for National Reconstruction in the Period of Transition to Socialism', ibid., p. 61.

20 'Vietnam to invite Sihanouk to visit Hanoi', AFP, Pattaya, Thailand, 29 August 1991.

21 'Cambodian Party Drops Communism, Backs Democracy', *International Herald Tribune*, 19 October 1991.

22 'Cambodians explain party changes to Vietnamese communists', AFP, Phnom Penh, 29 October 1991; Jacques Bekaert, 'Long Live the Party',

Bangkok Post, 22 November 1991; Michael Williams, 'An End to Cambodian Communism?', BBC World Service Commentary, 21 October 1991. Nguyen Duc Binh is now considered the senior ideologue in the Vietnamese leadership; he was formerly head of the party school. See Nayan Chanda, 'Hard-Liners Shape Role of Vietnam Reformers', *The Asian Wall Street Journal Weekly*, 8 July 1991.

23 Kavi Chongkittavorn, 'Veteran Vietnam envoy ends 11 year tenure in Phnom Penh', *The Nation*, 13 November 1991.

24 See Chanda, *Brother Enemy*, p. 379.

25 Ibid.; William J. Duiker, *Vietnam Since the Fall of Saigon*, Ohio University Press, Athens, Ohio, 1990, pp. 145–222. Ideological differences between the two countries were also marked at this time. Vietnam, which saw the Soviet Union as the leader of the socialist camp, was bitterly opposed to the Chinese concepts of hegemonism and the 'three worlds'. I am grateful to Carl Thayer for this observation.

26 Chanda, *Brother Enemy*, p. 190. The list of demands presented by Han Nianlong in April 1979 included the withdrawal of Vietnamese forces from Cambodia, mutual opposition to 'hegemonism', Vietnamese recognition of Chinese sovereignty over the Paracels and Spratlys, and permission for Vietnamese Chinese who had fled to China to return home.

27 Brantly Womack, 'China and Vietnam: peace at last?', *The World Today*, vol. 47, no. 10, October 1991, pp. 164–6; Leifer and Phipps, *Vietnam and Doi Moi*, pp. 27–8; and 'Read their lips', *The Economist*, 29 September 1991.

28 Interviews with Vietnamese and diplomatic sources, Hanoi, November 1991.

29 Kathleen Callo, 'Vietnam sends two top men on secret trip to China', Reuters News Agency, Hanoi, 29 July 1991; Nicholas D. Kristof, 'Hanoi leaders to visit China as ties revive', *New York Times*, 13 September 1991; 'China says normal relations on the agenda', Reuters, 11 September 1991.

30 See 'Vietnamese Leaders' Visit to China', BBC *Summary of World Broadcasts* (hereafter *SWB*), Part 3, FE/1222 A3/1, 6 November 1991; 'Sino-Vietnamese Accords Mark "New Beginning"', BBC *SWB*, FE/1224, 8 November 1991; Nayan Chanda, 'Beijing overhauls foreign policy goals', *Asian Wall Street Journal*, 5 November 1991; 'China relations normalised', *Vietnam Investment Review*, 11 November 1991.

31 'Vietnam's Relations with China Improve', BBC *SWB*, FE/1326 A3/1–2.

32 Michael Leifer, *ASEAN and the Security of South-East Asia*, Routledge, London and New York, 1989, pp. 63–4, 73–5.

33 Ibid., pp. 85–6; Chanda, *Brother Enemy*, pp. 318–20.

34 See Jeffrey Race and William S. Turley, 'The Third Indochina War', *Foreign Policy*, vol. 38, Spring 1980, pp. 92–118.

35 'Vietnam and Indonesia Sign Accords Marking End to Hanoi's Isolation',

International Herald Tribune, 22 November 1990.

36 Murray Hiebert, 'Steps to a Summit', *FEER*, 3 October 1991, p. 15; for the text of the Bali treaty see Leifer, *ASEAN*, pp. 170–74 and his comments on pp. 64–9.

37 Murray Hiebert and Michael Vatikiotis, 'ASEAN's Embrace', *FEER*, 14 November 1991; Moon Ihlwan, 'Singapore to Normalise Ties with Vietnam', Reuters, Singapore, 31 October 1991; 'Singapore's view of Indochina', *The Nation*, 27 November 1991. The invitation to Lee was confirmed in interviews in Hanoi, November 1991. See also 'Lee denies accepting VN offer', *The Nation*, 24 November 1991, and 'Lee considering becoming adviser to Vietnam', *Bangkok Post*, 25 November 1991; 'Prime Ministerial visits cement South East Asian relations', *Vietnam Investment Review*, 4 November 1991. In April 1992 Mr Lee paid a week-long visit at the invitation of the Vietnamese government.

38 I was surprised at the depth of these feelings in interviews in Hanoi, November 1991.

39 On his return to Bangkok, General Suchinda said that he had invited Vietnam to observe Thai military manoeuvres and had discussed the exchange of US aircraft spare parts held by the Vietnamese for Chinese manufactured tank parts held by Thailand. AFP and Reuters, Bangkok, 8 November 1991; Murray Hiebert, 'Building a Rapport', *FEER*, 30 January 1992.

40 Statement of the Thai Foreign Minister Arsa Sarasin to Reuters, Bangkok, 8 January 1992. During the visit of the Thai Prime Minister to Hanoi the two countries reached agreement on cooperating to end 'cut-throat' rice pricing. The two countries are the world's largest rice exporters after the United States. 'Thailand and Vietnam to cooperate on rice pricing', AFP, Hanoi, 13 January 1992.

41 See Jonathan Friedland, 'Twisting the Knife', *FEER*, 31 October 1991.

42 Jean-Pierre Langellier, 'M. Roland Dumas a regretté la lenteur du processus de démocratisation', *Le Monde*, 27 November 1991; *Vietnam News*, 25 November 1991; *Bangkok Post*, 26 November 1991. On German aid see *Vietnam News*, 21 November 1991, and *The Nation*, 24 November 1991.

43 'German junior FM arrives in Vietnam for repatriation talks', AFP, Hanoi, 14 January 1992.

44 On this issue see David Ennals, 'Must Vietnam still suffer?', *The Times*, 16 January 1990; *Vietnamese Migrants in Hong Kong*, Foreign and Commonwealth Office Background Brief, London, November 1991; and Kathleen Callo, 'Vietnam to take deported boat-people from ASEAN', Reuters, 31 October 1991.

45 Vietnam News Agency, 10 January 1992; AFP, Hanoi, 10 January 1992; and Associated Press, Bangkok, 13 January 1992.

46 *Cambodia: An Australian Peace Proposal*, Department of Foreign Affairs

and Trade, Canberra, 1990.

47 'Australia to resume trade and direct aid to Vietnam', Reuters, Canberra, 9 October 1991.

48 'Japanese Traders Cautiously Return to Vietnam', *International Herald Tribune*, 15 August 1990; 'Japanese gearing up for investment in Vietnam', *Bangkok Post*, 25 November 1991; 'Japanese business delegation visits Vietnam', AFP, Hanoi, 31 October 1991.

49 'Japan to send mission to Vietnam as first step to resuming aid', Reuters, Tokyo, 6 January 1992; 'Japanese government delegation arrives in Vietnam', Reuters, Hanoi, 14 January 1992; interviews with Japanese officials, Bangkok, November 1991.

50 Chanda, *Brother Enemy*, pp. 136–68, 263–96; see also Frederick Z. Brown, *Second Chance: The United States and Indochina in the 1990s*, Council on Foreign Relations, New York, 1989, pp. 21–32.

51 Brown, *Second Chance*, p. 82.

52 Ibid., pp. 109–14.

53 See Keith Richburg, 'Back to Vietnam', *Foreign Affairs*, vol. 70, no. 4, Fall 1991, pp. 111–31; and Leifer and Phipps, *Vietnam and Doi Moi*, p. 30.

54 Patrice de Beer, 'Première rencontre des ministres vietnamien et americain des affaires étrangères depuis 1973', *Le Monde*, 2 October 1990; Mark Tran, 'US-Vietnam talks mark policy thaw', *Guardian*, 29 September 1990.

55 Richburg, 'Back to Vietnam'; see also 'Vietnam's American conditions', *The Economist*, 27 April 1991; and 'Hard bargain for Hanoi', *The Times*, 27 April 1991.

56 'Washington and Hanoi Narrow Gap', *International Herald Tribune*, 23–24 November 1991; 'US, Hanoi hold first talks on normalisation', *Bangkok Post*, 23 November 1991. In interviews in Hanoi, several Vietnamese officials expressed disappointment with the pace of US/Vietnamese relations, one describing the leadership as 'furious' with the roadmap.

57 'For MIA Pact, US to Send Hanoi Aid', *International Herald Tribune*, 6 March 1992.

58 'Western Nations Urge Aid for Vietnam', *International Herald Tribune*, 17 October 1991; Kathleen Callo, 'Vietnam Welcomes US Move to Normalise, But Wants No Conditions', Reuters, Hanoi, 24 October 1991.

59 In a television hookup interview with journalists in Hong Kong in October 1991, Richard Solomon repeated US opposition. See 'US is Opposed to Pact by UK and Vietnam on Refugee Repatriation', *International Herald Tribune*, 19 October 1991.

60 Richburg, 'Back to Vietnam', highlights the role of a core group of policymakers in Washington, many of whom, like National Security

Adviser Brent Scowcroft and Assistant Secretary of State Lawrence
Eagleburger, were involved in the Vietnam war during the Nixon and Ford
administrations. See especially p. 127: 'For those working in the State
Department and the White House in the early 1970's, the highlight of their
careers was the opening of diplomatic relations with Beijing; the low point
was the humiliation of American helicopters lifting off from the roof of
the embassy in Saigon.' Congressman Chet Atkins, among others, has
accused present administration officials of still fighting the Vietnam War:
'They are using our Vietnam policy to settle old scores.' See also Lawrence Malkin, 'US Still Hostile to Hanoi', *International Herald Tribune*,
13 April 1990.

Chapter 6: Conclusions

1 Interview with Vo Van Kiet in BBC2 TV Assignment, 10 March 1992.
2 Interview with Professor Nguyen Thai Ninh, Chairman of the Ideological
   Commission of the Central Committee of the Vietnamese Communist
   Party, Hanoi, November 1991.
3 For a notable exception to this see Roderick MacFarquhar, 'The Anatomy
   of Collapse', *The New York Review of Books*, 26 September 1991.
4 See Karen Dawisha, *Eastern Europe, Gorbachev and Reform*, Cambridge
   University Press, 1990; Judy Batt, *East Central Europe from Reform to
   Transformation*, Royal Institute of International Affairs and Pinter,
   London, 1991, pp. 22–8.
5 Carlyle Thayer, 'Political Developments in Vietnam: From the 6th to 7th
   National Party Congress', October 1991.
6 Keith Richburg, 'Vietnamese rice production joins the big league',
   Guardian, 21 April 1990.
7 Author's observations and interviews during a visit to the Cao Dai centre
   at Tay Ninh, November 1991.
8 'Political Report of the Central Committee at the 7th National Congress'
   in *Communist Party of Vietnam 7th National Congress: Documents*,
   Foreign Languages Publishing House, Hanoi, 1991, p. 8.
9 'Vietnam Party Needs Urgent Reform, Official Says', Reuter, 13 January
   1992; 'Vietnamese Communist Party admits membership decline', Agence
   France Presse, 13 January 1992.